Cycling in Devon & Cornwall

Philip Routledge

Published by Sigma Leisure – an imprint of
Sigma Press, 1 South Oak Lane, Wilmslow, Cheshire SK9 6AR, England.

British Library Cataloguing in Publication Data
A CIP record for this book is available from the British Library.

ISBN: 1-85058-493-1

Typesetting and Design by: Sigma Press, Wilmslow, Cheshire.

Cover photograph: Tranquillity on the Bere Peninsula

Photographs and maps: the author

Printed by: MFP Design & Print

Disclaimer: the information in this book is given in good faith and is believed to be correct at the time of publication. No responsibility is accepted by either the author or publisher for errors or omissions, or for any loss or injury howsoever caused. Only you can judge your own fitness, competence and experience.

Preface

'Cycling in Devon and Cornwall' is the second in my series of books based on the following simple philosophy: leisure cycling is a gentle and healthy pursuit to be enjoyed by all who care to participate without consideration of age, experience or fitness.

The book will guide you to some of the very best cycling opportunities in these two spectacular and immensely varied counties. It shows you the best way to begin an exploration of the south west peninsula and gives excellent clear directions and interesting descriptions of the individual routes and surrounding locations. Cycle paths are included for those who are not 'in the know' and these, along with a few short forest routes are ideal for picnic and family trips.

As well as enjoying a pleasant cycle ride and some healthy exercise, cyclists will draw equal satisfaction from other aspects of the ride. These may be an industrial archaeological connection, a look at some rare wildlife or simply some particularly beautiful views or surroundings.

Every route in 'Cycling in Devon and Cornwall' can be enjoyed by literally anyone who can ride a bike, from the raw novice to the superfit sports rider. Each route is guaranteed to produce a worthwhile return for the effort put in.

Devon and Cornwall have more coastline than any other two counties in Great Britain.They have high moorland, charming old towns, rocky coves, golden beaches, patchwork green countryside and a maze of little lanes. Add a pleasant climate and more sunshine than any other region in Britain and all these factors work together to create absolutely perfect conditions for leisure cycling.

Philip Routledge

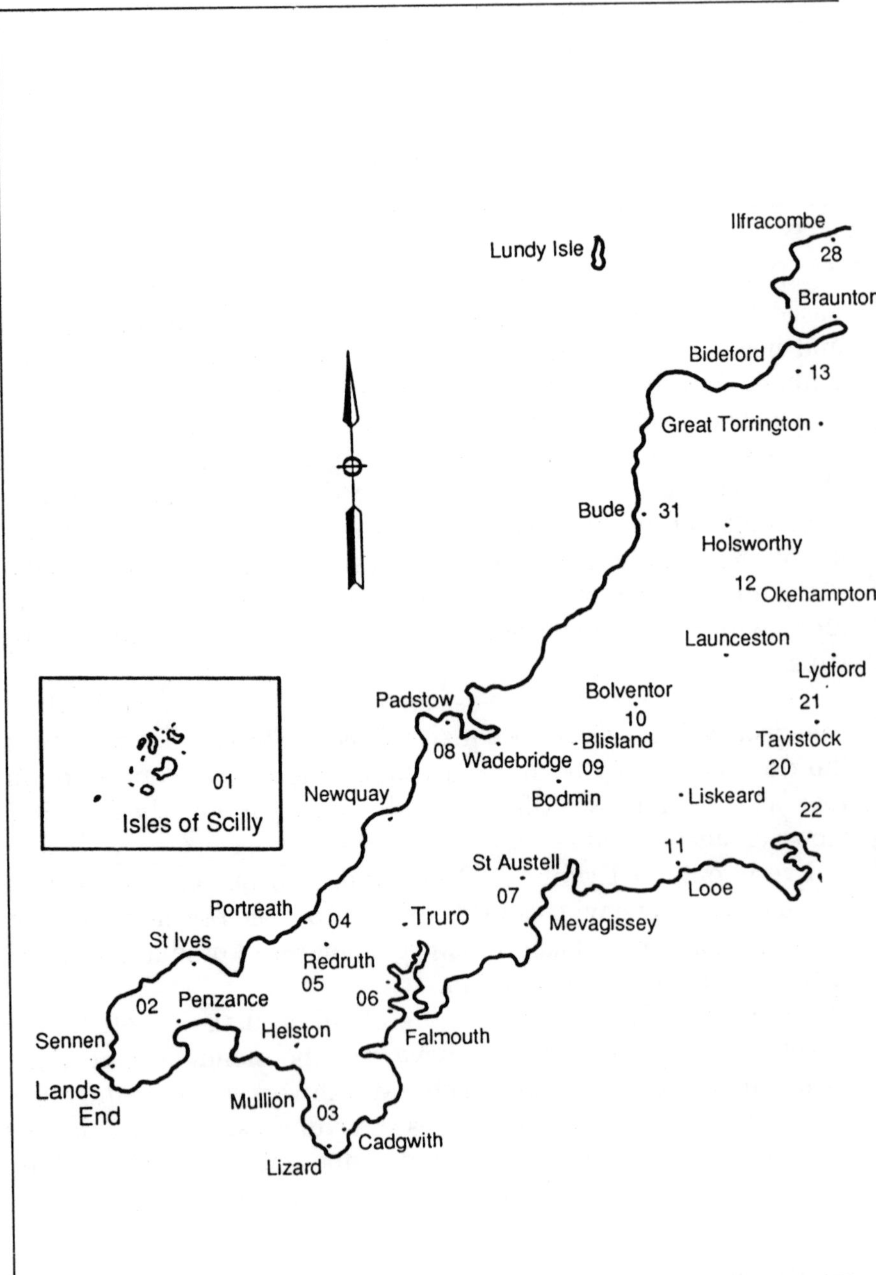
Ilfracombe
28
Lundy Isle
Braunton
Bideford
13
Great Torrington
Bude
31
Holsworthy
12
Okehampton
Launceston
Lydford
Bolventor
10
Padstow
21
Tavistock
Blisland
08
Wadebridge
09
20
Isles of Scilly
01
Newquay
Bodmin
Liskeard
22
11
St Austell
07
Looe
Portreath
04
Truro
Mevagissey
St Ives
Redruth
05
06
02
Penzance
Helston
Falmouth
Sennen
Lands End
Mullion
03
Cadgwith
Lizard

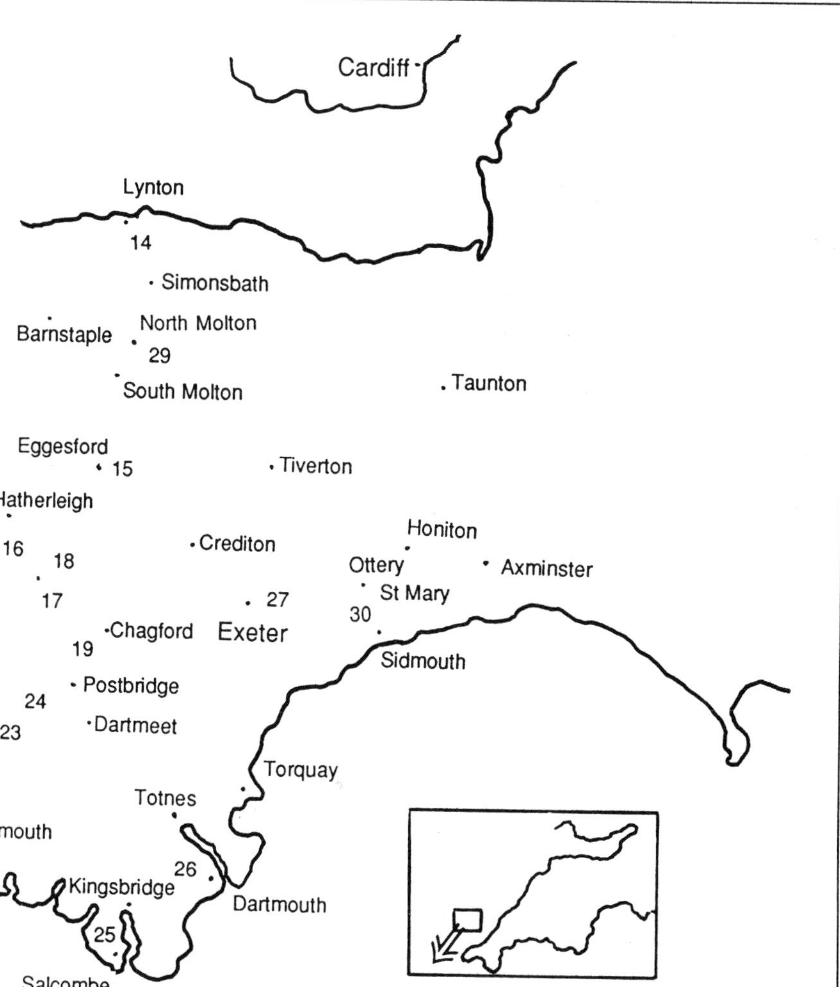
Cardiff
Lynton
14
Simonsbath
Barnstaple
North Molton
29
South Molton
Taunton
Eggesford
15
Tiverton
Hatherleigh
16
18
17
Crediton
Honiton
Ottery
St Mary
Axminster
27
30
Chagford
Exeter
19
Sidmouth
Postbridge
24
23
Dartmeet
Torquay
Totnes
Plymouth
26
Kingsbridge
Dartmouth
25
Salcombe

Contents

Introduction

Devon and Cornwall, these two most western English counties preserve the natural ambience of a basic landscape in a way that has been lost in more developed parts of the land.

Nearly 500 miles of unspoilt coastline, Dartmoor, Bodmin Moor and part of Exmoor. Tantalising famous names such as Lamorna, Hope, Tintagel and Zennor. Lakes, pockets of sub-tropical splendour, wild cliff tops and sandy coves. Cobbled harbours, green lanes, ancient seafaring cities and stately homes. Where do we start?

There is more coastline and more fresh air than any other region of Britain. There are few inland points of Cornwall which are more than twenty miles from the sea and Dartmoor sits brooding in the heart of Devon, forcing the green patchwork to the edges.

The rides in the book will show you a more intimate Devon and Cornwall. You may find a few hidden secrets, discover a little village church or find a new insight into living conditions of country folk in the eighteenth century. The rides will help you discover endless small points of fascination, sometimes the simplest things which will bring the real Devon and Cornwall to life for you in a way that is satisfying, private, personal and very different way to the perception of modern tourism.

The pace of life is slow and relaxing. The people are kind, considerate and friendly and you will find a welcome wherever you go. The coastal and high moorland scenery is spectacular, the wildlife is everywhere and the scented wild flowers will line your path in a magnificent show of colour. Devon and Cornwall still preserve some of the most unspoilt countryside in Europe, award-winning uncrowded beaches and the very best of English cuisine.

We live in a 90mph world and the gentle pace of the bicycle provides an unusually fortifying tonic. With our eye-line on a par with a walker and our progress at the speed of a top class runner, we can see over hedges to enjoy the landscape and wildlife whilst making real headway and covering real distances in a reasonable span of time and all for little effort. Whilst we are doing this, we are benefiting from the form of gentle exercise that is very much the dish of the day in modern medical research.

On some rides, you might be greeted by the sea. This may be in the form of some delightful cove; it may be a bustling little harbour or perhaps, a beach of golden sand. On other rides you will be delighted by soft rolling greenery and unspoilt villages, well away from any heavy traffic and towns. Maybe you will decide to experience the wildness and grandeur of Dartmoor or the mystical interior of Cornwall or maybe a mixture by riding out of the cities of Exeter or Plymouth and into another secret world beyond which simply could not be discovered any other way than by bicycle in such a short time.

Take plenty of time to stop and enjoy your surroundings. You might want to take a wholesome packed lunch with you when you ride or you may prefer to sample the joys of a country pub; you should have no trouble finding one.

The rides are carefully planned to avoid steep climbs wherever possible and to keep away from traffic unless it is absolutely unavoidable for a very short distance. None of the rides are difficult but there is a good choice of distance ranging from the simplest leg stretcher-for the kids to a good full day's tour. Enjoy your riding, take care and good luck with the weather.

Equipment

- ☐ Additional equipment translates to additional weight.
- ☐ Additional weight translates to additional effort.
- ☐ Hills, especially upward hills, and head winds magnify the undesirable effects of additional weight.

Bearing these simple rules in mind and on the assumption that your bike has pedals, wheels and security equipment, there are really only a few simple accessories worth considering. These are as follows:

The **bell** might well be fitted to your bike anyway. If it is not do not worry, you can always sing, cough or loudly clear your throat, but a bell is easier. It is associated with cycling and it is inoffensive.

The **frame corner pack** is useful because it is dedicated to carrying your **puncture kit**, basic **tool kit** and **first aid** equipment. Once it is packed, you can virtually forget about it but it will be there when needed. Keep the tools to a minimum, on most bikes, two Allen keys, a multi spanner and a cross head screw driver are sufficient.

Your puncture repair kit is not much use without a **pump**.

A back (or front) rack is so useful, I cannot imagine being without one.

A Single or Double Lightweight Pannier enables you to carry spare clothing, sandwiches, cool drinks, and anything else which you may require.

You'll know why you need a **front spray deflector** the first time you try to ride on a wet or muddy surface.

Security

A sad story: lock it or lose it – and don't leave it outside at night. If you are leaving your bike out of sight, particularly in towns and cities, **do** lock it or you **will** lose it. It is a sad state of affairs, but according to crime prevention statistics, the chances of an unguarded and unlocked bicycle being stolen, in the busy central area of a town the size of Swindon, would be greater than 50% over a 48 hour period. The chances of a **locked** but unguarded bicycle being vandalised or having pieces taken off it (like wheels!) during periods of darkness are greater than 30% over the same period. In other words, you are more likely to lose your bike than you are not to lose it, so here are a few simple tips:

Use a "D" lock around the frame, through the rear wheel and onto the most solid object you can find. A lot of towns and cities now have proper cycle parking arrangements. Most commonly these are 'Sheffield stands', strong 'n'-shaped metal stands which are specially designed for bicycle locking. If possible secure your front wheel, even if it means carrying another locking device.

Make sure that you have a photograph of your bicycle and a note of any serial numbers or distinctive markings and carry this with you. Use special invisible ultraviolet markers and write your name or post code on the bike. By doing this and having the descriptive information readily available, at least you can give the police a chance.

Just in case the worst does happen, always make sure you are carrying your bus fare to get home. A long walk after the indignation of losing your bike will dim even the brightest spirit.

Safety

- ☐ Keep off busy roads whenever possible.
- ☐ Be safe, be seen. Lights at night. Fluorescents by day.
- ☐ Ring your bell when approaching pedestrians.
- ☐ Wear helmets for rough, off-road riding.
- ☐ Make sure that your bicycle is properly maintained.

Buying a Bicycle

Apart from colour and budget, there are some deciding factors when buying a bicycle and these notes will hopefully offer a few tips.

The correct type of machine for you and your budget. There are several clearly definable types of bicycle and each has its own particular advantages and disadvantages. Here is a brief list of the major options along with the pros and cons of various categories.

Mountain Bike (also known as MTB or ATB). Pro: go anywhere. Very easy to ride, very manoeuvrable. Con: poor for long distance touring or speed work.

Roadster (The traditional vicar's bike): Pro: solid, hub gears. Will probably last for ever. Con: heavy and very hard to pedal up hill, which is probably why vicars usually push.

Shopper (Small-wheeled lightweight bicycle. Mainly for the ladies): Pro: easy to ride, easy to store. Hardly ever stolen. Con: no good off-road and not much better on-road.

Folding Bike (One for the boater?). Pro: transportable in tiny spaces such as car boots, canal boats, yacht tenders, buses or trains. Great for the urban jungle. Con: limited in its overall ability by its tiny wheels and compromised design.

Quality Touring Bicycle: (Often seen loaded with panniers) Pro: A quality touring bicycle is a joy to ride and a joy to own. Long distance riding can be carried out in comfort. The best all round bicycle to own. Con: Quality does not come cheap. Really rough stuff should be left to the ATB's.

Hybrid (Half mountain bike, half tourer) Pro: lighter and more comfortable than a mountain bike. Better on tarmac. Con: limited off-road ability.

Sporting Bicycle (Thin rimmed wheels, drop bars) Pro: can be faster than a tourer. Con: not as comfortable or as strong as a tourer. Horrible on anything but billiard-table surfaces.

Road Racing Bicycles (Thin rim wheels, quality lightweight frames) Pro: ultimate speed depends how much you are willing to pay. Expensive, specialist racing bicycles are a beauty to behold. Con: unless you are road racing or training for road racing, these machines are useless.

Owning a Bicycle

Owning a bicycle should be a great pleasure and a good bicycle, well maintained and well cared for, will prove to be a friend for life. Like most things, ownership of a bicycle can be as expensive or as cheap as you care to make it.

Service Schedules If you are using your bicycle regularly and you are not confident in carrying out your own servicing, an annual service at a reputable cycle dealer is a great investment.

Insurance Insurance is very much a matter of personal choice and personal circumstance. It is not compulsory and often you will be buying cover that you already have in another form. If you have one, check the terms of your house insurance policy and look into the possibility of paying a small extra premium for your cycling needs if necessary.

Cleaning By cleaning your bicycle regularly you will achieve three things. Firstly it will look better, secondly it will operate more smoothly and thirdly you will become aware of faults before they develop into serious problems. Use warm soapy water and be certain to oil the chain and gears after the water has dried off. Wash carefully around the brakes and around the gear sets.

The Cyclist's Essential Check List

It is good practice to carry out the following quick checks each time you set out.

- ☐ **Tyres** Inflated, good tread.
- ☐ **Tools** Basic appropriate tools carried plus the pump.
- ☐ **Adjusted** Are the saddle and the handlebars set at the correct height and rake?
- ☐ **Spare tube** and puncture repair kit.
- ☐ **Security** 'D' lock or good chain carried.
- ☐ **Lubrication** Have you oiled your chain recently? Every fifty miles, after washing or rain, or every two weeks when in use.
- ☐ **Lights** Will you need them?
- ☐ **Ingredients** Food and water if required.
- ☐ **Clothing** Check the weather.
- ☐ **Condition of the bicycle** A final look over your bicycle. Check your steering, brakes and gears.

Insects, the Sun and the Wind

Insects a good insect repellent is an essential requirement, especially on hot summer days.

Sun take the appropriate precautions of sun protection cream.

Wind do not underestimate the effect of the wind. A good tailwind can take a great deal of the effort out of cycling, a strong headwind, conversely, will require a much greater effort than still wind conditions. If you are planning to cycle and return along the same leg, tackle the upwind direction first and you will then be able to look forward to an easier return trip.

Dress Sense

If you are likely to be riding along busy roads, in towns or at night, make sure you can be seen – wear a brightly coloured cycle helmet, shirt, anorak etc.

In rain, there are two schools of thought and depending on which one you subscribe to, you will either get wet or you will get hot. The decision to put on waterproofs or get wet is always difficult to get right and initially, if you are undecided, put the waterproofs on as soon as the rain starts because once you are wet, the waterproofs will only hold the moisture in.

Hiring

The wide availability of cycle hire centres has happily created a situation whereby you do not need to own a bicycle to enjoy the routes in this book. Use some basic common sense when hiring and consider the following points:

Charges it is up to you to decide if the charges are fair or not, but do be sure that you know exactly what you are expected to pay. Some hirers quote by the hour, some by the day and some by the week, so take care. Shop around if you can.

Deposits do not leave your car keys. Effectively, your car is held as a deposit and this is disproportionate. All hirers will, quite reasonably, insist on some form of identification. A driving licence, a credit card or a passport are usually acceptable either solely or in combination.

Transporting Your Bicycle By Car

There are several methods and each has pros and cons:

Roof rack clamp fittings Pro: security, less possibility of damage to the bicycle. Con: low bridges. putting the bicycle on and taking it off.

Back Rack Pro: very easy to use. Cheap to buy. Con: poor security when the car is unattended. Can knock the bicycles about if you are carrying more than one.

Tow Bar Rack Pro: good security, you can 'D' lock your bike to your car. Ease of use. Con: you need a towbar.

There are pitfalls to beware of. Here are a few:

If you have any fast-fix, clip-on equipment such as pumps, drinking bottles, mudguards, pannier sets or anything else that is not welded or screwed to the bicycle, take it off or it will certainly fall off.

If you are carrying your bikes by the roof rack method, beware of car park barriers...

Bicycles carried transversely on racks, on the backs of the cars, are generally wider than the car itself. If you are travelling along narrow lanes or through tight town streets, allow for that extra bit of width.

If you are transporting your bicycle on a back rack, make certain that your bicycle tyres are well clear of the car's exhaust. The hot exhaust gases can melt the tyre.

Railways, Buses, Aeroplanes and Ferries

Two of the pleasure cyclist's greatest allies are the tailwind and the downward gradient. Unfortunately some of the basic laws of mathematics and geometry dictate that whatever goes up must come down and whatever blows one one way does not blow back the other way half an hour later when you happen to want to return. The answer to your dilemma may well lie in a bit of pre-planning and a railway station or a bus stop.

Railway Travel The services offered to cyclists by train operators are constantly changing, especially in view of the turmoil of reorganisation within the railway industry. For latest information check before you plan to travel and always expect to book because space is limited. In broad terms, most train operators are helpful and well disposed towards cyclists but demand can be high.

On journeys where changes of train are required, you will normally be expected to be responsible for moving your own bicycle but this would probably be advisable under any circumstances. Remember these rules and you should be OK:

☐ Book before you go. (There may be a £3 fee)

- ☐ Long distance trains such as sleeper services and Intercity services will have an overall capacity for forty bicycles.
- ☐ Sprinters have space for four bicycles per pair of carriages.

If in doubt, keep smiling because conductors have discretion beyond these limits if space allows.

Bus Travel Buses are best used to 'get back home' or 'get back to a parked car' having secured your bicycle in some safe place for later retrieval. It is easy to check local timetables and plan a day's cycling on this basis and a fantastic way to use a good tailwind!

Facilities offered by bus operators for carrying bicycles by bus tend to be fairly sketchy in terms of both detail and availability. There are however a few facilities available for bicycles. In these cases, the costs are usually very high although some operators actually offer free passage for bicycles. In all cases enquiry and pre-booking are essential.

Ferries There several useful ferries in Devon and Cornwall. With estuaries slashing up the coastline and a number of scattered islands, ferries form an essential part of the infrastructure. See the note in Ride 1 concerning the *Scillonian*. The charges that the operators deem fair for bicycle ruin the economics of a short visit with your own bike and the only really sensible way to enjoy a short cycling trip to the Scillies is by hiring when you arrive.

Major estuary ferries in the region include: the Torpoint Ferry (Plymouth), the two Dartmouth ferries, the Fowey to Bodinnick Ferry on the Fowey River and the King Harry ferry on the River Fal. These are much more reasonable in their attitudes to bikes with charges varying from nothing to just a little more. The Padstow to Rock ferry and the St Mawes to Falmouth ferry will also carry your bike subject to availability of space.

Air Travel Most major airlines will carry bicycles either within your luggage allowance or at a small additional charge. Some airlines supply special bags free of charge. On pressurised aircraft, ensure that you deflate the tyres otherwise they may explode at altitude due to the low atmospheric pressure in the hold.

Summary There is a vast range of transport services on offer for cyclists within the public domain but availability is almost always subject to booking. The golden rule is simple. Book and enquire before travelling!

Common Notices and Waymarks

There is a multitude of information available to cyclists in the form of waymarks and notices. These can be rings or signs, fixed to the street furniture, they can be bits of painted wood, nailed to walls or wired to trees. There are waymarks carved in stone, painted on the tarmac, stencilled onto wood, routed into posts and set in concrete and there are all combinations of styles and materials. I am sure that these are not the only forms that I have seen on my travels, but it will give you an idea.

It would be nice to believe that waymarking of a route is consistent in its format and presentation, but be warned, it is not. Just because you have seen a run of twelve wooden posts with yellow tops and a routed message saying 'Cycle Path' does not mean that the next post is not blue concrete with the message 'Bikes' and buried in the back of the hedge. Beware of practical jokers who take delight in turning pointers to send you the wrong way; try to verify the route, especially in or near urban areas where petty vandalism may occur.

Keep a constant lookout for waymarks and try to find a pattern; it will greatly enhance your enjoyment of the ride. If you do come across any vandalism, try to report it to the responsible authority so that they may include the problem in their work schedules.

Rights of Way

In England, you are forbidden access to land unless you are granted some right waiving the landowner's rights. This may come in the form of a public footpath, a bridle way, a highway or a permissive route. Canal towpaths and most railway paths are good examples of permissive routes.

Generally, common sense will guide you along if you lose the way. If in doubt, keep to well used and established paths, look out for evidence of cycle tracks and follow your front wheel.

Ride 1

Island Exploring on St Mary's, Isles of Scilly

An island paradise of patchwork fields and winding lanes.

Maps: Landranger 1:50,000 series. Sheet number 203.

Distance: A return ride exploring the various coastal points will be approximately 7 miles (11 km).

Waymarked: No.

Gradients: No steep climbs.

General surface description: Tarmac/stone tracks.

Future proposals: N/A

Other cycle routes linking: No cycle routes link but there is excellent cycling on the 'off islands' of Tresco and St Martins. Connections can be made by the regular ferry and trip boats. Bicycles can be carried by agreement.

Bicycle hire: It is advisable to pre-book your hire bike. They are available on St Martins, St Mary's and Tresco. There is a substantial charge for carrying your own bicycle on the Scillonian (equivalent to about four days bike hire, the aircraft and helicopter are not equipped to accommodate bicycles.

Shops and refreshments: The main commercial area is Hugh Town. It is advisable to carry food and drink elsewhere, although there are many isolated cafés and stores.

Special comments: Although the ride is on public roads, traffic is extremely light and generally slow moving. Despite this, follow the 'be seen' rules. The 'A' roads are much quieter than most minor roads on the mainland.

Special warnings: You will not want to come home.

Permits: N/A

This is a ride around one of the most beautiful and unspoilt parts of Great Britain, a tiny 1554 acre island situated 28 miles west of Land's End and forming the last bastion of England before the wild expanse of the Atlantic Ocean. The Isles of Scilly (or Scilly as known locally) are a microcosm of modern society, having their own farms, schools, medical centres, councils, airport and a self-supporting economy which is broadly based on tourism and fresh flowers.

The population of Scilly is approximately 2350 and of these approximately 2000 live on St Mary's. The network of tiny gentle patchwork fields slopes down to the very accessible coastline which can easily be explored. There are numerous deserted sandy beaches and magical rocky coves which are can be accessed by simple paths or short scrambles. Bathing is mainly safe in the shallow waters but beware of the eastern coast around Pelistry Bay where swirling currents can be hazardous for the unwary.

Hugh Town is the charming capital of Scilly and stands on a narrow strip of land enveloped by two natural harbours and under the protection of the old garrison post at Star Castle. The granite buildings are well able to cope with Atlantic gales and within their thick walls are a good selection of shops, restaurants, pubs, banks and cafes to serve your every whim. St Mary's is one of the few places where it seems unnecessary to use a security lock for your bicycle. On a day-to-day basis, the bicycle is clearly the ideal form of personal transport for Scilly where motor vehicles seem to encroach on the natural peace.

Take plenty of time cycling around St Mary's; there is plenty to

Enjoying a picnic on the Isles of Scilly

see, plenty to do and it is an ideal place just to relax and forget about the world for a while. Visit the other islands if you have time by taking a boat from the quay in Hugh Town.

Access Points

A daily steamer service leaves Penzance in the morning takes 2 hours and 40 minutes to reach St Mary's. If you return the same evening you will have about 4½ hours ashore. A fixed-wing aircraft service operates from Lands End airfield and a helicopter service operates from Penzance Heliport. The steamer offers the cheapest service, the helicopter the most expensive.

The Route

1. From the quay in 'Hugh Town', turn left towards the town's shopping area.
2. At a fork in the town centre turn left if you are in a clockwise mood or right if you are in an anticlockwise mood.
3. Assuming you have turned left you will be leaving 'Hugh Town' on the A3111 with Porth Mellon Beach on your left. If you were in an anticlockwise mood you will have to read the directions backwards from the bottom which is extremely difficult, but it serves you right for being in a funny mood.
4. Take the first left towards Porthloo, passing Newford Island and Taylor's Island on your left.
5. After approximately one kilometre follow the road as it bends around to the right with the golf club on your left.
6. Turn left at the T junction towards the radio mast, go straight ahead for Bar Point or go right by the coastguard station to continue.
7. After another kilometre carry straight on if you want to visit Watermill Cove or go right towards Maypole to continue.
8. At the T junction turn left onto the A3110 towards Pelistry Bay.
9. As the road bends right, continue straight ahead for a break on the beach at Pelistry Bay, opposite Toll's Island (beware of the

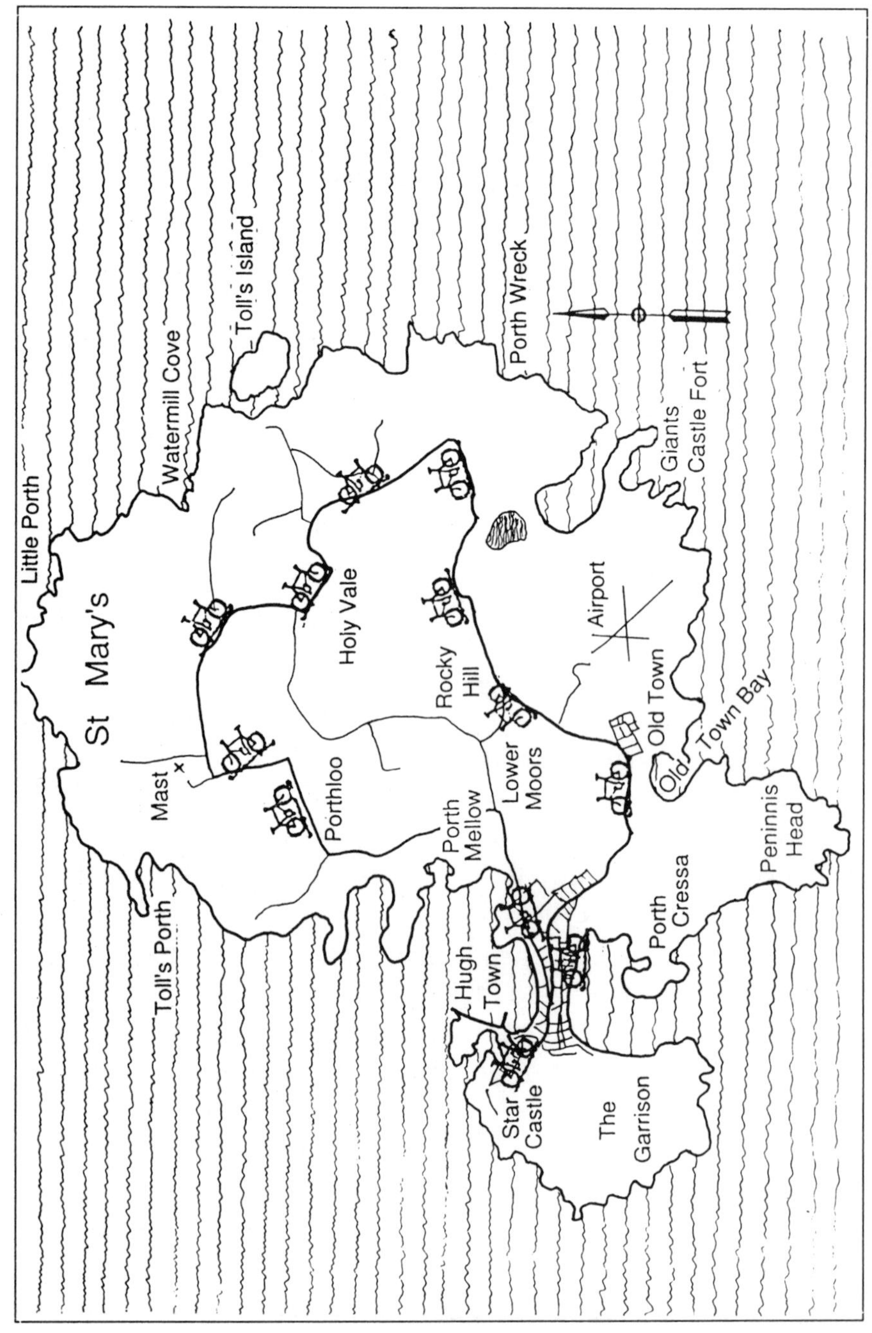
Little Porth
Watermill Cove
Toll's Island
Porth Wreck
St Mary's
Holy Vale
Rocky Hill
Airport
Giants Castle Fort
Old Town
Old Town Bay
Mast
Porthloo
Lower Moors
Porth Mellow
Peninnis Head
Porth Cressa
Toll's Porth
Hugh Town
Star Castle
The Garrison

swirling sea currents here if you swim). To continue, follow the road around to the right.

10. Continue past the airport to return to Hugh Town via the A3112 through Old Town and Old Town Bay.

Nearby

Nothing happens very fast in Scilly but what does happen is well regimented. For instance, the trip boats that leave the harbour in St Mary's leave bang on time, plying their routes, weaving between the Islands through the hidden deep-water channels. An uninformed observer, watching the boats from some position on shore, may think that the steersman is not paying attention, or is away from his station collecting tickets, such is the apparent randomness of the boat's course on what appears to be a uniform sea. What the observer cannot tell from this perspective is the maze of shallow protrusions, poking up just a few feet below the surface. Only the experienced steersman can find a route through such waters without dragging the bottom out of the boat or stranding fast on some godforsaken pile of seaweed-covered rock or sandbank.

Bishops Rock is the most westerly landfall in the British Isles and is the home of Britain's tallest lighthouse. It stands like a sentry above the Atlantic, 175 feet above the waves. It has a 2.6 million-candle-power light which is clearly visible from a range of nearly 30 miles at sea level. The current lighthouse was built when an earlier cast-iron structure succumbed to the sea in 1850. It was heavily strengthened with a new outer lining in 1881 and has remained unchanged since then, apart from the addition of a helipad in 1976.

Ride 2

A Magical Tour of Western Cornwall from Penzance to Land's End

A magnificent semi-coastal, semi-rural ride based on Land's End and Penzance. Sights along the way include Newlyn, Lamorna Cove, Mousehole, Sennen Cove, Drift Reservoir and a host of little-known sleepy villages.

Maps: Landranger 1:50,000 series. Sheet number 203.

Distance: Total return ride 31 miles (45 km).

Waymarked: No.

Gradients: A few short sharp climbs and descents out of the coastal centres, otherwise a remarkably level ride.

General surface description: Tarmac.

Future proposals: N/A

Other cycle routes linking: N/A

Bicycle hire: Penzance

Shops and refreshments: Numerous opportunities along the route

Special comments: N/A

Special warnings: Watch out for traffic and *be seen!* Unavoidably, some of very short stretches of the route are along the A30 and other short stretches use 'B' roads. Happily, most of the route is via very quiet country lanes.

Permits: N/A

This fascinating on-road circular ride will take you to parts of the far west of Cornwall that are rarely visited by the mass of tourists in the region as well as visiting the beautiful cove at Lamorna and the old harbour at Mousehole. This exposed and wind-blown peninsula has an unusual beauty of its own. Almost up to your approach to the tourist mecca of Land's End, your route will be on remarkably quiet country lanes.

This is a fairly energetic but very worthwhile ride for which you should allow a full day in order to enjoy plenty of sightseeing along the way. If it is a hot day, take your swimming gear; there are several good bathing opportunities. The high point of the ride is a visit to beautiful Sennen Cove and Land's End but the route takes you past some of the most interesting and spectacular scenery in the whole of Cornwall.

Land's End is one of the world's most famous landmarks. Its local coastal landscape displays a timeless wild beauty which is somehow in keeping with its special significance as the most westerly mainland point of Britain. Myth and legend abound; on a balmy sunny afternoon it is not difficult to imagine scenes from the ancient past. It is beyond here that the legendary land of Lyonesse is supposed to have sunk into the sea; perhaps it will rise again one day. These are headlands that have reputedly born witness to the exploits of King Arthur and his knights and before him great Celtic Chiefs were undoubtedly here looking wonderinglyrously out to sea and dreaming of an unknown world beyond. In more recent times there are numerous tales of smugglers sneaking ashore in the dead of night and of evil wreckers setting false beacons to passing shipping.

Land's End is probably most famous for its association with John O'Groats. Countless brave individuals have started or ended the 874

Only one way to go from here!

mile (1406 km) journey from here, some for the sheer challenge and others for the benefit of charity. Modes of transport have varied. The best known and possibly the most popular method is ordinary walking. Some have tried to walk backwards whilst others have taken to wheeled bathtubs, unicycles, vintage vehicles, lawn mowers, pogo sticks and perhaps less spectacularly bicycles. (With good planning, the cycle ride to John O'Groats can be done in three weeks although some extremely energetic cyclists have done the trip in just one week.)

Access Points

This ride is based on Penzance Railway Station where there are excellent car parking facilities nearby. If you want to start the ride from Land's End, there is good affordable car parking in Sennen Cove. (Parking at Land's End includes the entrance fee to the attractions there. Only if you are intending to visit these attractions as well as making the ride, would this be the better place to park.)

Mousehole would be another good alternative starting point and there is a good car park on the edge of the village.

The Route

1. Turn Left out of Penzance Railway Station and follow the A3077 coastal road west signed to Newlyn and Mousehole, passing the car parks, the harbours and the sea front on your left.
2. Keep on the coast road through Newlyn signed to Mousehole.
3. Follow through Mousehole village, keeping on the coast road. DO NOT take the right turn which is signed to Lamorna as this will take you inland. Keep to the unsigned coast road.
4. Some distance out of Mousehole, go left at the 'T' junction signed to Lamorna and Castallack and continue along this road following signs to Lamorna.
5. At the 'T' junction go left to visit Lamorna Cove and then return past the junction following the signs to Penzance and Land's End.

6. At the 'T' junction with the B3315 go left, signed to Land's End Porthcurno and St Buryan.
7. Follow the B3315 for just over a mile and then turn right opposite an old stone cross signed to St Buryan.
8. In the centre of St Buryan, go left opposite the church and follow this road out of the village, signed to Logan Rock Porthcurno and Land's End.
9. At the next junction, turn right (signed Crean) and follow this road through Crean to the hamlet of Bottoms.
10. Take the first right as you go into Bottoms – an unmarked narrow lane.
11. After following this lane for a while, go left at the 'T' junction.
12. Just before reaching the A30, go left by a small settlement of some modern dormer houses. Follow this lane back into the countryside.
13. Go right at the 'T' junction with the B3315.
14. At the 'T' junction, go left along the A30 for the short distance to the Land's End complex.
15. Leave the Land's End complex along the A30 and turn left at the Sennen Cove junction if you wish to visit this charming little resort.
16. Continuing along the A30, turn left along the B3306 signed to St Just Pendeen and Land's End Aerodrome.
17. Immediately after passing the aerodrome, turn right along the unmarked lane towards the hill. Continue winding along this road for a while.
18. At the 'T' junction, turn right.
19. Continue along this road towards Sancreed.
20. At the 'T' junction, turn right along the road signed Drift and Penzance. Continue past the church.
21. Follow this road past Drift Reservoir to the crossroads with the A30.

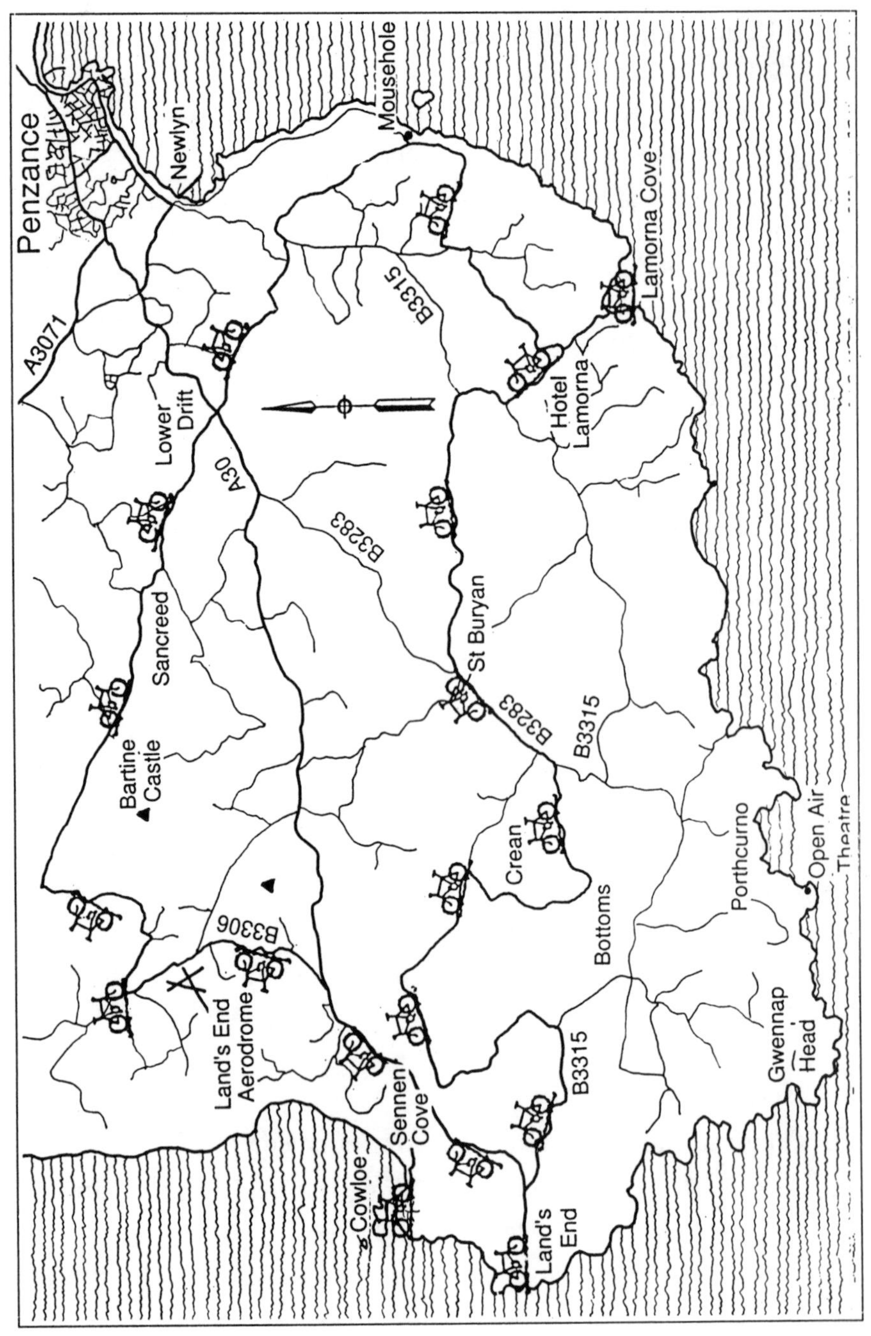
Penzance
Newlyn
Mousehole
Lamorna Cove
A3071
B3315
Lower Drift
Hotel Lamorna
A30
B3283
St Buryan
Sancreed
B3283
B3315
Bartine Castle
Crean
Porthcurno
Open Air Theatre
B3306
Bottoms
Land's End Aerodrome
B3315
Gwennap Head
Sennen Cove
Cowloe
Land's End

22. Go straight across the A30 into the narrow lane signed to Chyenhal.
23. At the junction with B3315, go left towards Penzance.
24. This road comes out in Newlyn from where you should retrace your route along the sea front to Penzance Station.

Nearby

The haven and artists' colony of St Ives is situated on the north coast and is well worth visiting. St Michael's Mount, in St Michael's Bay east of Penzance, can be accessed by causeway at low tide or by boat at high tide. The bustling town of Penzance and Britain's busiest fishing harbour at Newlyn are both very interesting and everywhere can be seen remains of the great Cornish tin-mining industry which formed part of the very roots of the Industrial Revolution.

Ride 3

The Lizard Peninsula, South West Cornwall

A 26-mile round trip, mainly on very quiet back lanes around England's most southerly peninsula.

Maps: Landranger 1:50,000 series. Sheet numbers 203 and 204.

Distance: Total return ride 28 miles (45 km) including a visit to Kynance Cove.

Waymarked: No. All of this ride is on quiet public roads.

Gradients: Only climbing out of the coves. The bulk of the ride is surprisingly level.

General surface description: Tarmac.

Future proposals: N/A

Other cycle routes linking: N/A

Bicycle hire: Helston.

Shops and refreshments: Plenty of opportunities along the route. There is a good choice in Lizard Village.

Special comments: N/A

Special warnings: N/A

Permits: N/A

The Lizard Peninsula culminates in Lizard Point, the most southerly mainland point in Great Britain. The spectacularly rocky coastline plays a large part in forming the character of this ride, which dips in and out some of Cornwall's prettiest coves. Indeed, the ride begins and ends in Cadgwith Cove, which is considered to be one of the prettiest coastal villages in the county.

On the ride, you will cross Goonhilly Downs with its famous Earth Station, a telecom facility for linking into geo-stationary satellites. You will also pass a farm of graceful wind generators which will hypnotise you if you stare at them too long. Further along you will pass sandy Poldhu Cove and then Mullion Cove, which will put you in the mood for smuggling. Church Cove, near Lizard Point is notable for its thatched cottages and peaceful charm.

Lizard village

At Lizard Point itself, you can briefly be the most southerly person on mainland Great Britain. Achieving this accolade is a popular and competitive pastime. Watch carefully and you will see that virtually everybody tries to achieve it and you may suspect that most try to pretend that they are simply looking at the view. If the competition proves too fierce, you may be willing to settle for a lesser achievement. Perhaps you will settle for the accolade of being the most southerly person in Britain wearing a blue hat or riding a pink bicycle? If you still have the energy, Kynance Cove is worth the detour; it is set in magnificent National Trust surroundings.

Access Points

There is good affordable car parking in Cadgwith Cove. The route is described with its starting point here but there is no reason why you should not start from anywhere along the route, including Kynance Cove, where there is a good car park. The Lizard would be another good alternative. The directions are anti-clockwise to avoid as many right-hand turns as possible.

The Route

1. From the 'pay and display' local authority car park just above the cove and village of Cadgwith, turn left, downhill to Cadgwith Cove and harbour. If the air is clear you will like the view ahead. Spend a little while admiring the scene.
2. Continue through Cadgwith and a short sharp ¼ mile climb will set you onto level ground in the village of Ruan Minor.
3. Continue to the crossroads on the edge of the village and turn right, (signed to Kennack Sands).
4. Pass through the village of Kuggar and after a short distance, turn left along the road to Coverack and St Keverne.
5. Continue across Goonhilly downs and towards the eerie sight of several vast geo-stationary satellite tracking dishes which dominate the vast open expanse of these desolate downs.
6. At the crossroads with the B3293, turn left towards Helston and pass the main entrance to the Earth Station.
7. Turn left off the B3293 opposite the entrance to Trelowarren House.
8. Continue straight on past the wind farm.
9. At the crossroads with the A3083, continue straight ahead, (signed Cury and Mullion).
10. In Cury village, opposite the Jubilee Playing Fields turn left along the little one way Church Road and this will take you past a delightful old English Church.
11. Turn left again to resume your track.
12. Continue past Poldhu Cove and through Mullion, keeping left in the one way system and then following the signs to The Lizard.
13. About a mile outside Mullion you will come back to the A3083 opposite the Mullion Holiday Park.
14. Turn right and follow this road for a short distance before bearing left into the unmarked country lane.

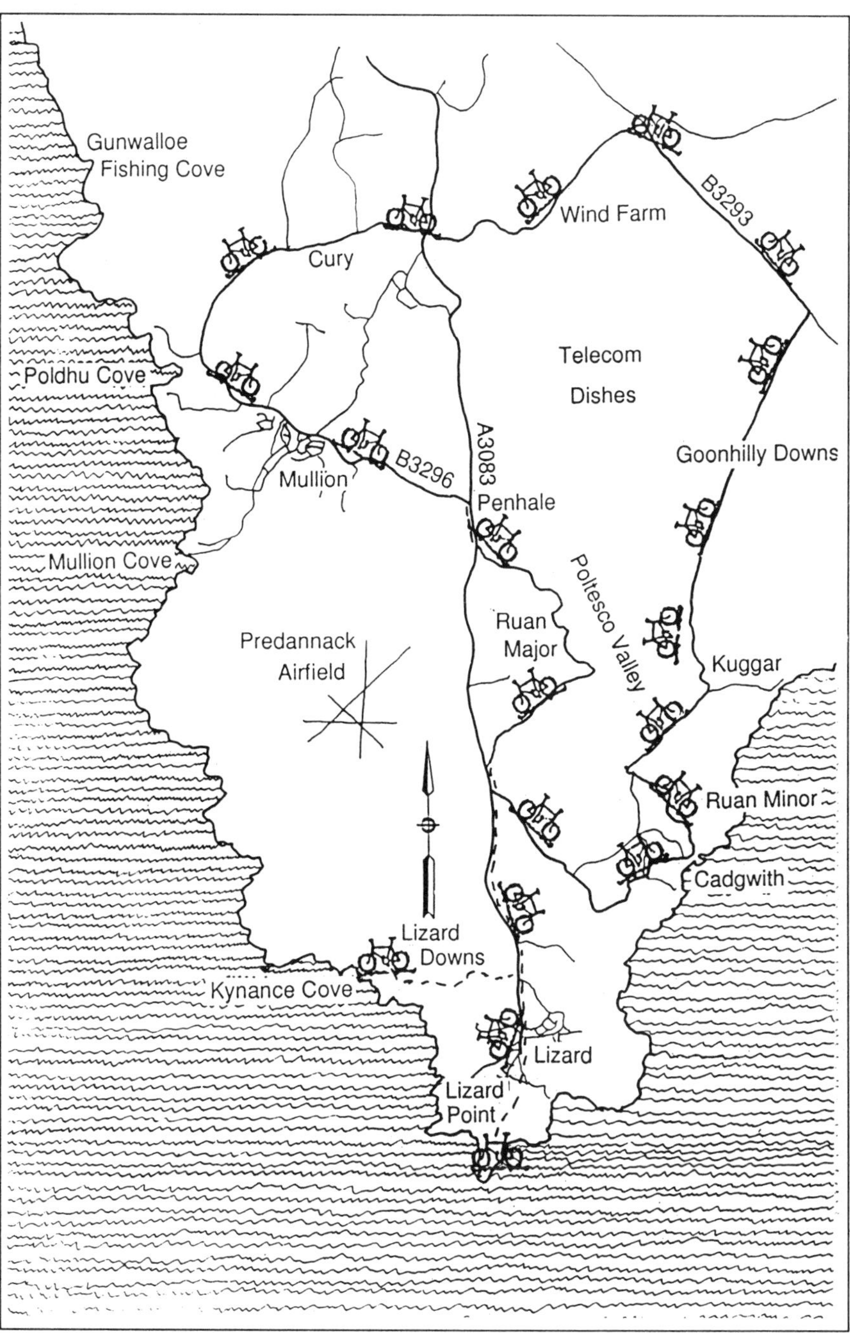
Gunwalloe
Fishing Cove
Cury
Wind Farm
B3293
Telecom
Dishes
Poldhu Cove
A3083
B3296
Mullion
Penhale
Goonhilly Downs
Mullion Cove
Poltesco Valley
Ruan
Major
Predannack
Airfield
Kuggar
Ruan Minor
Cadgwith
Lizard
Downs
Kynance Cove
Lizard
Lizard
Point

15. Follow this lane until you come to a right turn signed to Ruan Minor.
16. Take this turn and continue through a ford to a cross roads.
17. Carry straight ahead, keeping the Ebenezer Chapel on your right.
18. Carry on straight ahead for a short distance before turning left onto the A3083 for the final mile and a half into Lizard village.
19. ¼ of a mile after joining the A3083 you will see the turning to the left for Cadgwith. You will need to return to this road later to make your way back to Cadgwith Car Park, but first explore The Lizard, Church Cove, the lighthouse and Kynance Cove. You will manage this without directions.
20. Finally, upon returning to the Cadgwith turning off the A3083 continue for about ½ a mile to a sharp left-hand bend. Continue straight ahead here onto a minor road.
21. This road will bend and twist for a while before coming out on the edge of Cadgwith Village.
22. At the 'T' junction, you should turn right and then immediately right again between the old stone posts. You will find the car park a short distance along, downhill on your left.

Nearby

The Lizard Peninsula, for all its isolation and wildness, can probably boast more billions of pounds worth of high technology hardware per square mile than any other similar sized area in Europe. As well as a major wind powered generating plant, there are two very expansive Royal Naval air fields, the UK's prime satellite tracking station and an early warning radar capability that would wake the dead.

If you make a telephone call from an office in London to an office in New York, your call may be routed through Goonhilly Earth Station's powerful satellite transceivers. As you ride across Goonhilly Downs, you will see these giant dishes which range in size from big to enormous. In common with most high-tech equipment, the dishes have become smaller as advances have been made in computerisation and electronic amplification of the weak signals. The dishes that are carrying most of the telecommunication traffic are, therefore, the smaller ones. The latest dishes are actually capable of detecting signals of the equivalent intensity of a two-bar electric fire on the surface of the moon. Parts of the Earth Station are open to the public.

Royal Naval Air Station Culdrose and Royal Naval Air Station Predannack form the UK's premier naval helicopter training base. On a busy day, the natural peace and quiet of the peninsula is shattered by the constant beating noise of the big Sea King helicopters. If you see a flurry of helicopters operating at low level well out to sea, it is usually an indication that they are towing sonar equipment through the water to practice their anti submarine warfare techniques. This will normally coincide with passing submarines which may be setting out or returning from Atlantic patrol.

Goonhilly Downs are maintained by English Nature and offer a great deal of fascination for the botanist and geologist. The unique heath land supports the rare Cornish Heath and some of the small flowering plants cannot be found elsewhere. The large boulders or crusairs which are deposited across the heath are relics from the ice age.

Ride 4

Coast to Coast across Cornwall (Part One)

The Portreath Tramroad: Portreath to Crofthandy.

Maps: Landranger 1:50,000 series. Sheet numbers 203 and 204.

Distance: Portreath to Crofthandy one way 8 miles (13 km).

Waymarked Fairly well but in two formats. This may soon be standardised in the Portreath to Scorrier format, i.e. 'Portreath Tramroad' but there are some waymarks on the Scorrier to Crofthandy section which read 'Killifreth'. Each waymark is colour-coded and these translate as follows. Yellow = Public Footpath. Blue = Bridleway. Black = Public Road (or By-way). Red = Pure By-way.

Gradients: No serious gradients. (The horses managed OK and they were towing two-ton wagons!)

General surface description: Stony tracks. Mostly well drained with the occasional muddy section. Generally unsuitable for narrow-tyred tourers.

Future proposals: This is a Groundwork Trust project. The policy is constant improvement when funds allow. Eventually it is intended that this will form part of a grand tramway network of over 100 km in length. For up to date information contact Groundwork Kerrier at Old Cowlin's Mill, Penhallick, Carn Brea, Redruth, Cornwall. Tel: 01209 – 612917.

Other cycle routes linking: Ride 5 and (via back lanes) Ride 6. Tehidy Woods are also nearby (see note under 'Attractions').

Bicycle hire: Redruth.

Shops and refreshments: Plenty of places along the route.

Special comments: Worth taking a puncture repair kit and a spare inner tube. The trail is described by Groundwork Kerrier as an all weather, all year route. Stout clothing and footwear is recommended in wet or wintery conditions. The surface varies from tarmac on the roads through firm gravel on the recently refurbished parts to sections of potentially muddy but solid based track. Not all the route is off-road and care should be taken on some of short but possibly busy road sections.

Special warnings: N/A

Permits: N/A

This ride broadly follows a fascinating tramway path from the old North coast harbour of Portreath inland to the dereliction of the disused tin mines at the old coal yard at Crofthandy. To complete a coast-to-coast ride, after an optional exploration of the mining areas around Redruth and Camborne, (ride 6), the ride continues with a gentle descent through the Poldice Valley and by the Carnon River to Devoran and Point on the shores of Restronguet Creek. (ride 5).

The Portreath tramroad follows the disused route of the first surfaced tramroad to be built to serve the great copper and tin lodes of the region. A group of mine owners got together to build the tramway after struggling for too many years with the old technology of packhorse on rutted track. It opened in 1812 and the improvement in carrying capacity was monumental, one horse being able to haul the same weight of ore or coal as twenty pack horses could carry before.

Clear waymarks on the Portreath tramroad

The crushed ore was taken to Portreath harbour for shipping on to the smelters in South Wales. Coal to power the mighty Cornish steam engines, for pumping the mines, winding the shaft gear and stamping the product, was brought back on returning ships to Portreath and distributed throughout the area via the new tramway.

Although the advances made by the tramway were huge, they were short-lived. Around 1825 the rail-

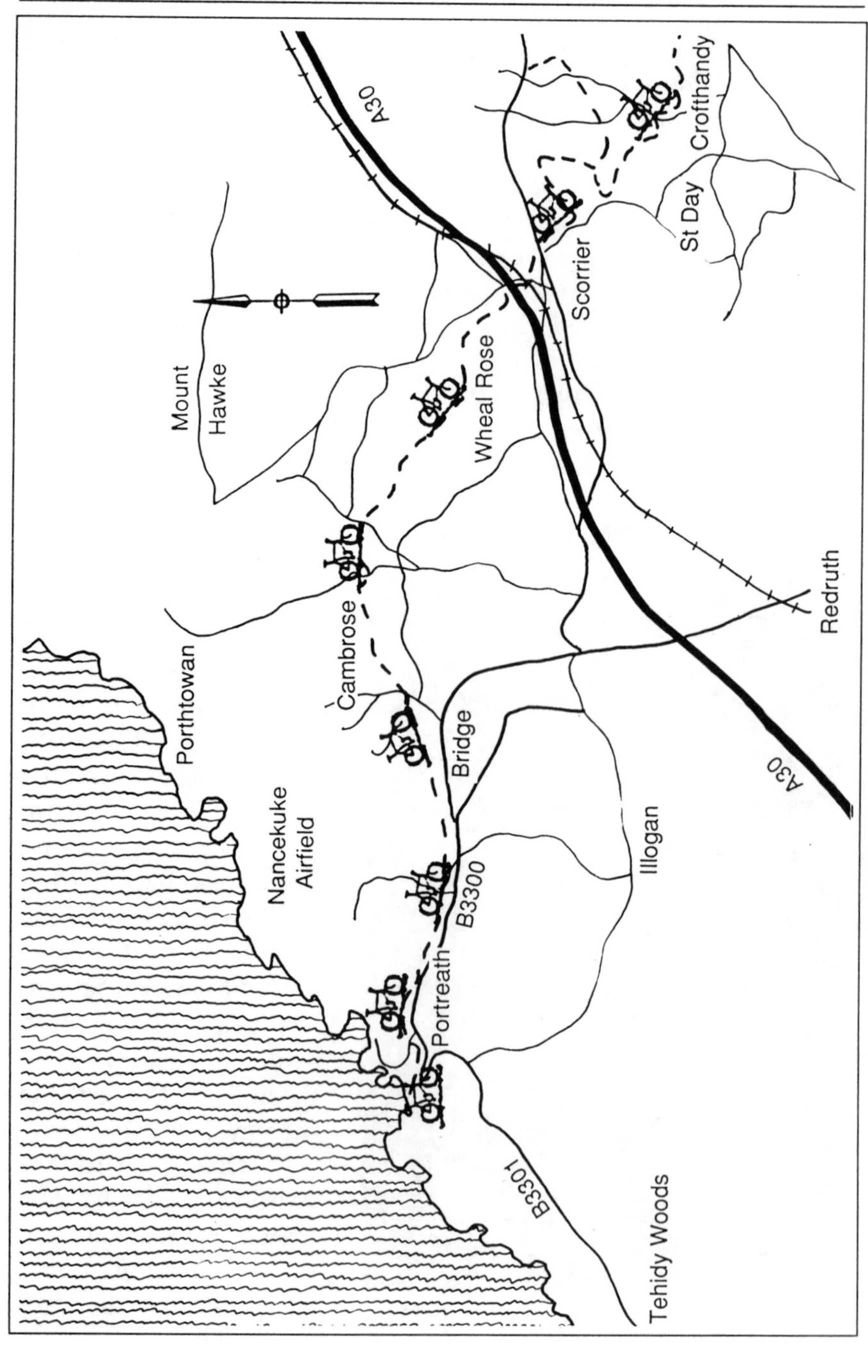
A30
Crofthandy
St Day
Scorrier
Mount
Hawke
Wheal Rose
Cambrose
Porthtowan
Redruth
Bridge
Nancekuke
Airfield
Illogan
B3300
A30
Portreath
B3301
Tehidy Woods

ways from Redruth, Devoran and Hayle as well as a new inclined plane in Portreath made the tramway more or less obsolete. Ironically, the linking ride to Devoran follows the course of the railway that was to take all of the cargo that the tramway had carried just a few years earlier.

The tramroad was reopened in 1994 and forms part of a trio of rides which, between them, form a fascinating coast-to-coast route. The whole of the Mineral Tramways Project, when completed, will be one of Europe's most extensive industrial heritage trails. Its network of old tramway routes will combine with old railway track-bed paths, to form a network of traffic-free trails over 100 kilometres in length.

The best place to start your exploration of the Mineral Tramways Network is the Tramways Centre at Old Cowlins Mill. This is situated south of the railway line behind the industrial estate by Carn Brea Leisure Centre and Homeworld, at the base of Carn Brea. Up to date information is well presented in a fascinating display which portrays the background of the tramways and railways which make up this exceptional network. Within the display is an explanation of the cycling facilities as will as various maps, photographs and drawings which will give you the latest picture.

Access Points

The starting point of the ride is Portreath Beach car park, but there is no reason why you should not start from Crofthandy. This would be a good alternative if you are planning a one way trip and prefer the idea of going slightly downhill.

The Route

1. From Portreath Beach car park head inland along the B3300 leaving the harbour on your left.
2. Just past the parade of shops on your right and the pub on your left, fork left along the residential road Sunnyvale Road.
3. At the top of this road, where it begins to curve right to rejoin the B3300, you will see the Portreath Tramroad waymarked

straight ahead. The waymarking from here is very clear and easy to follow.

4. Following the waymarks, the trail slopes gently and steadily upwards and crosses a minor road.
5. At the next road, the route is waymarked straight ahead where you will first join another very minor road from your left and then turn left after a few yards onto a busier minor road.
6. The finger posts will point you to the right after about half a mile.
7. Continue straight on at the cross roads into another very minor road.
8. At the 'T' junction, the route goes straight ahead, off-road again onto a waymarked track. Eventually you will emerge on a minor road just to the north of the A30. Turn right and cross the A30 on the road bridge.
9. Just beyond the bridge, you will be signed left to follow through a tiny tunnel under the railway.
10. After following the signs across the Chacewater road, you will be sent down a busy minor road towards St Day and Carharrack.
11. Watch out carefully for the finger posts sending you left onto a track which will take you to towards the barren wastes around the relics of the mines past Killifreth and onto the old coal yard at Crofthandy.

Nearby

The sight of old engine houses is never far away from the trail and it is easy to imagine the original loads being transported by the wobbly old wagons, tenuously held on course by the short plates of brittle cast iron that formed the rails with their crude "L" shaped section. In addition to the depth of industrial interest it is impossible to ignore the natural grandeur of the landscape most noticeable in very different ways at either end of the trail. Although the route to Devoran is not yet officially open or waymarked, it is easily passable and can make a most satisfying coast-to-coast route.

Portreath is now a beach resort, complete with an amusement arcade. It was once a busy port, serviced by the tramway that is now the Trail and later by an inclined plane from the 'new' railway, now itself long gone too, although the inclined plane is clearly visible on the western edge of the village. Portreath airfield was used in the '50s and '60s as a development and storage centre for germ warfare, although this is an activity which no longer takes place on the site.

Scorrier estate was the domain of the Williams family who were wealthy mine owners and party to building the tramway.

Redruth developed from a small farming town to a sprawling urbanisation nearly all as a result of tin wealth. When the tin market collapsed, Redruth saw some fairly bleak times.

Tehidy Woods. Just to the west of Portreath on the cliff top B3301 road is a car park for Tehidy Woods. Cycling is allowed in most parts of the woods. There is a very peaceful route winding through the old woodland to the old disused Tehidy Hospital and returning through the west of the woodland onto the Majestic North Coast Cliff tops west of the car park. The route is not waymarked but the woods are not very big so you will not get lost for long. There are few more magnificent cliffs than those which tower over the Western Atlantic Approaches on this part of the North Cornish coast.

Ride 5

Coast to Coast Across Cornwall (Part Two)

The Redruth and Chacewater Railway: Crofthandy to Point.

Maps: Landranger 1:50,000 series. Sheet numbers 203 and 204.

Distance: Point to the old coal-yard at Crofthandy one way 6 miles (10 km).

Waymarked: Planned for the future. It is proposed that waymarks shall be colour coded: Yellow = Public Footpath. Blue = Bridleway. Black = Public Road (or By-way). Red = Pure By-way.

Gradients: No serious gradients. A gradual slope down to the coast.

General surface description: Stony tracks and tarmac roads. Generally unsuitable for narrow-tyred tourers.

Future proposals: This is a Groundwork Trust project. The policy is constant improvement when funds allow. It is intended that this will form part of a grand tramway network of over 100 km in length. For up to date information contact Groundwork Kerrier at Old Cowlin's Mill, Penhallick, Carn Brea, Redruth, Cornwall. Tel: 01209 – 612917.

Other cycle routes linking: Ride 4 and (via back lanes) Ride 6.

Bicycle hire: Redruth.

Shops and refreshments: Plenty of places along the route.

Special warnings: N/A

Permits: N/A

This route forms part of a trio of rides – see Ride 4. The ride makes a gentle descent through the Poldice Valle' and by the Carnon River to Devoran and Point, on the shores of Restronguet Creek. Throughout the ride you will be passing in one form or another, through the scars of an industrial past. The Poldice Valley has acre upon acre of dead land devoid of normal vegetation and unnatural in form and shape. Strange conical steel wire shapes mark the uncapped tops of mine shafts, some of which employed dozens of men and boys underground; women and girls (the famous 'Bal Maidens') sorted and broke up the mineral-bearing rock. There was dirty, difficult and dangerous work for all. At one time this valley would have been teeming with activity, steam trains plying their noisy way up and down from Restronguet creek, horses and carts rumbling here and there and hundreds of men, women and children making their way to and from the works at the changes of shift.

Although the advances made by the Portreath Tramway (Ride 4), in the transportation of product from the Great Flat Lode mines to the north coast were huge, they were short lived. Around 1825 the railway from Redruth to Devoran made the tramway more or less obsolete and introduced Devoran as a busy port at the head of Restronguet Creek.

Access Points

The starting point of the ride is the old coal yard at Crofthandy. You can also start from Point which would be a good alternative if the wind was strong both from the south or east. The Redruth and Chacewater Railway originally ran from a point south of Redruth through the Crofthandy area and down the Poldice and Carnon River valley to Devoran. It linked via the Portreath Tramway to the north coast at Portreath and via the Great Flat Lode complex to Gwithian north of Camborne.

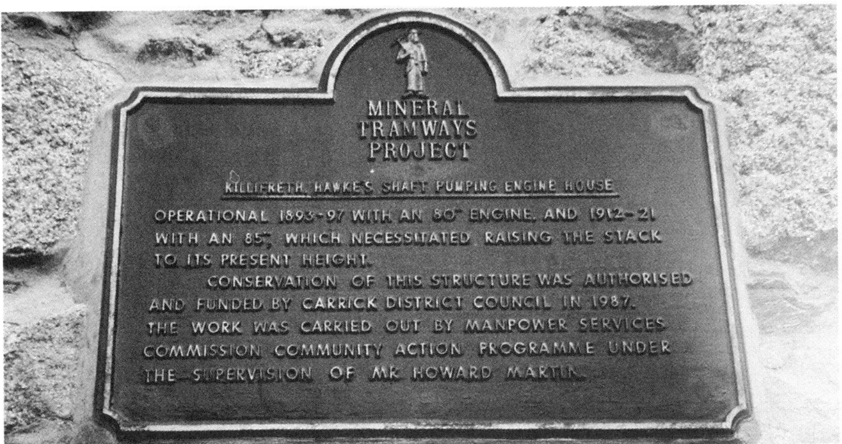

Information plaque on the tramroad

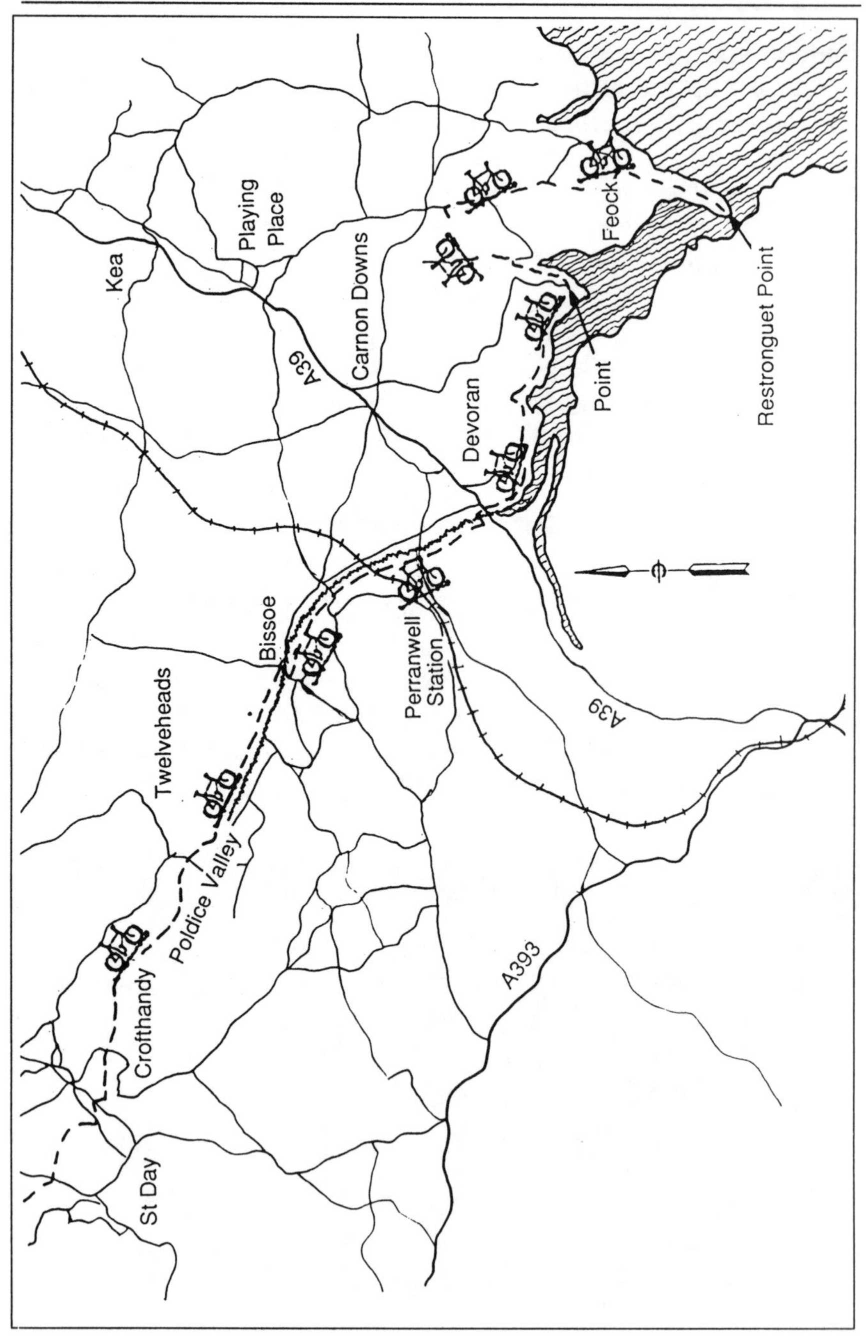
Playing Place
Kea
Carnon Downs
A39
Feock
Restronguet Point
Point
Devoran
Bissoe
Perranwell Station
A39
Twelveheads
Poldice Valley
Crofthandy
A393
St Day

The Route

1. From Crofthandy follow the Poldice Valley to the south keeping on the tracks on the right of the stream bed.
2. The valley eventually becomes a little narrower and leads out onto a minor road.
3. Carry straight ahead down the road for about fifty metres and then turn left onto the bridleway to continue the descent of the valley. Keep the stream well below you on your right-hand side.
4. Continue along the track until you emerge onto a much busier road in Bissoe.
5. Turn left and follow the road for a short distance.
6. After passing the concrete works on the right, turn right down the very minor road.
7. A few metres along this road, turn left along the made-up cycle/walking path. You will pass the settling ponds for the poisoned Carnon River.
8. Follow the path, crossing two minor roads and one very busy minor road after a high railway viaduct.
9. After crossing the Carnon River on a wooden bridge, you will emerge onto the horribly busy A39.
10. Go left and carefully cross the road. (This crossing of the A39 can be particularly nasty, so please take care).
11. Turn right into the bottom of Devoran Village.
12. The creek opens up on your right as you follow the roads through Devoran and on to Point. To find your way simply keep on the road as close to the creek as possible.

Nearby

Devoran Village was a sleepy little fishing and farming community until it suffered the surprise onslaught of the arrival of the Redruth and Chacewater railway around 1825. Overnight, ships began visiting Devoran and the place became a busy industrial port. The process has now gone full circle and the original sleepy atmosphere has returned.

Ride 6

A Diversion from the Coast to Coast across Cornwall (Part Three)

A Circular Ride on the Great Flat Lode.

Maps: Landranger 1:50,000 series. Sheet numbers 203 and 204.

Distance: Circular route from the old coal yard at Crofthandy around the Great Flat Lode and return to the old coal yard at Crofthandy 15 miles (24 km).

Waymarked: 'Great Flat Lode'. Waymarks are colour-coded and these translate as follows. Yellow = Public Footpath. Blue = Bridleway. Black = Public Road (or By-way). Red = Pure By-way.

Gradients: No back breaking gradients but a few ups and downs.

General surface description: The surface varies from tarmac on the roads through firm gravel on the recently refurbished parts to sections of potentially muddy but solid based track. Not all the route is off-road and care should be taken on some short but possibly busy road sections. Generally this ride is unsuitable for narrow-tyred tourers.

Future proposals: This is a Groundwork Trust project. The policy is constant improvement when funds allow. Eventually it is intended that this will form part of a grand tramway network of over 100 km in length. For up to date information contact Groundwork Kerrier at Old Cowlin's Mill, Penhallick, Carn Brea, Redruth, Cornwall. Tel: 01209 – 612917.

Other cycle routes linking: Ride 4A and Ride 4B can be accessed via old tramroads and back lanes. For further (up to date) details contact Groundwork Kerrier.

Bicycle hire: Redruth.

Shops and refreshments: Plenty of places near the route.

Special comments: Worth taking a puncture repair kit and a spare inner tube.

Special warnings: N/A

Permits: N/A

The ride follows a circular route around the 'Great Flat Lode', a fascinating insight into the now virtually-defunct deep mining for copper and tin that formed the backbone of the area's prosperity.

These old industrial areas, around Redruth and Camborne are

riddled with dereliction and recent efforts Groundwork Kerrier have begun to bring the remains to life and interpret their archeological history.

This ride forms part a trio of rides – see Rides 4 & 5 – and is largely based on the old tramroads that served the great installations of the metal mining industry. It traces the derelict winding and pumping engine houses and the great 'stamps' (ore crushing plants), all of which were powered by mighty Cornish steam powered beam engines. The final route of the ride is yet to be established but essentially follows a course around the base of Carn Brea. The route information is slightly changeable and therefore latest information should always be obtained from Groundwork Kerrier until the final waymarked route is established.

The 'Great Flat Lode Circular Ride' derives its name from the geological characteristic of the main vein of ore which sits like a great slab under the whole area (A 'lode' is a vein of metal ore and the vein that yields the metals in this region is, in a geological sense, large and flat, hence the name.).

Access Points

The starting point of the ride as described here is the Kerrier Groundwork headquarters at Cowlin's Mill, south of Carn Brea. (See future proposals entry in information panel). You could also start from Crofthandy end and make a cross country link onto the Great Flat Lode. This is the eventual aim of the project and up to date information should be obtained from Groundwork Kerrier. Car parking is not normally a problem at either point.

The Route

The route is in the process of being waymarked and negotiations are still taking place in respect of certain rights of way. Groundwork Kerrier are constantly improving and updating the exact route and will be happy to supply up to date route information from their headquarters at Cowlin's Mill.

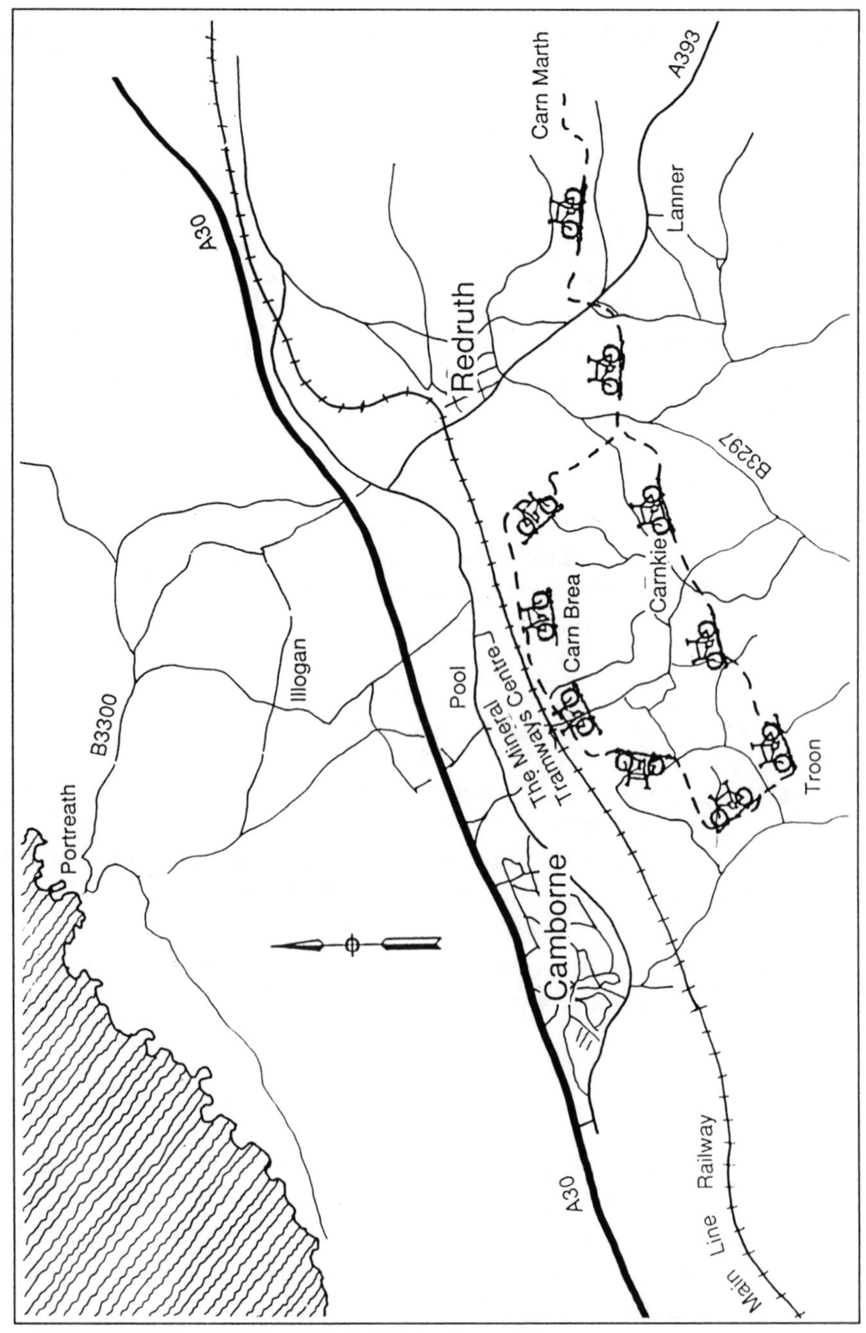
Carn Marth
A393
Lanner
A30
Redruth
B3297
Carnkie
Carn Brea
Illogan
Pool
The Mineral Tramways Centre
B3300
Troon
Portreath
Camborne
A30
Main Line Railway

Nearby

In addition to the depth of industrial interest it is impossible to ignore the strange unnatural grandeur of the dereliction and the extent of the damage suffered by the landscape.

The Poldice Valley and areas around St Day, Carharrack, Redruth and Camborne are all surrounded by the scars of metal mining and although the industrial archeologist may view the scene with a certain amount of fascination, in real terms it represents nothing less than an ecological disaster. St Day was once described as the richest square mile on Earth but it certainly does not give that impression now.

Only a few miles away at St Austell is the ecological disaster that is fondly described as the 'China Clay Area'. Giant mounds of white silica and sand dominate the landscape in a way that would make a team of lunar astronauts feel at home. Certain experts argue that a great deal of the material contained in the waste mounds is suitable for construction and road building purposes if certain compromises were accepted and financial constraints were less rigorous.

Rough riding below Carn Brea

Ride 7

Carlyon Bay and Pentewan

South of St Austell, South Cornwall – a Return Ride.

From the sands of Carlyon Bay past the tall ships at Charlestown Harbour to the pretty coves at Lower Porthpean and Pentewan, returning via a peaceful cycle trail down the Pentewan Valley.

Maps: Landranger 1:50,000 series. Sheet number 204.

Distance: Total return ride 12½ miles (20 km).

Waymarked: Partly.

Gradients: A few climbs, each of less than ½ a kilometre.

General surface description: Mainly tarmac or concrete. The cycle trail is well drained consolidated stone and the bridleway section between the Cottage and the Hospice can be fairly muddy in wet conditions. Narrow-tyred touring bikes should avoid this bridleway section in wet weather.

Future proposals: The cycle trail from Pentewan will eventually be extended to the north and into the area of the china clay tips that can be seen on the northern horizon. Eventually this section may be linked to the Camel trail at Bodmin which will create a fabulous coast-to-coast (Pentewan to Padstow) ride.

Other cycle routes linking: None at present (See future proposals).

Bicycle hire: Pentewan Village end of the cycle trail.

Shops and refreshments: Carlyon Bay, Charlestown, Porthpean, Pentewan, London Apprentice.

Special comments: N/A

Special warnings: N/A

Permits: None required.

This is a fairly easy half day or day ride which takes you to some of the finest sands in this part of Cornwall as well as visiting the charming old harbour of Charlestown where you will normally be able see a selection of tall ships as well as visiting the excellent

Through the trees on the Pentewan Valley trail

Charlestown Shipwreck and Heritage Centre. The route will also take you to Pentewan, which has an excellent beach, and along the Pentewan Valley Cycle Trail before returning to Carlyon Bay.

It is hoped that the Pentewan Valley Cycle Trail will one day be extended into the china clay areas north of St Austell and from there on to Bodmin to link up with the Camel Trail. This will create an exceptional coast-to-coast route which, when considered with the existing route between Portreath and Point, will surely make Cornwall the envy of the leisure cycling world.

This is a ride which can easily be divided into two or three sections to suit your time schedule and energy reserves. If you only want a short ride it would be sensible to base your starting point at Pentewan. The surroundings are truly magnificent and because of difficult car parking, the area is not crowded either in terms of people or traffic.

Access Points

There is a large car park at Carlyon Bay Leisure Centre, the starting point of this ride. To find this, turn off the A390 onto the A3082 between St Austell and St Blazey Gate. After a short distance on the A3082, you will see a private road on your right signed Carlyon Bay Hotel and Leisure Centre. Follow the signs and you will arrive in the large car park.

As an alternative, if you simply want to try a short and safe ride on the Pentewan Valley Cycle and Leisure Trail (an excellent choice if you have small children), there is car parking just south of London Apprentice off the B32723 or in Pentewan Village.

The Route

1. Leave the Carlyon Bay Leisure Centre car park on Beach Road (the ramp road out the car park).
2. Continue straight ahead through the residential area. You pass a new car garage and a small parade of shops before arriving at a mini island.
3. Continue straight ahead here along Church Road, signed Charlestown.
4. After passing St Paul's Church go left at the 'T' junction onto the A3061 towards Charlestown Harbour.
5. If you want to explore Charlestown, continue straight ahead here, if not..
6. Turn Right into Duporth Road signed Duporth and Porthpean.
7. A gradual climb will take you to a 'T' junction where you should continue straight ahead leaving the sports ground and hospice on your left.
8. After about 200 metres, you will see some concrete bollards on your left which mark the entrance to a bridleway. Take the bridleway and follow downhill for about five hundred metres.
9. Just after passing a cottage, you will emerge onto a tarmac road. Turn left and follow this road, which will soon change to a wide unsurfaced bridle track.
10. Follow this track until you emerge through a gate to a 'T' junction.

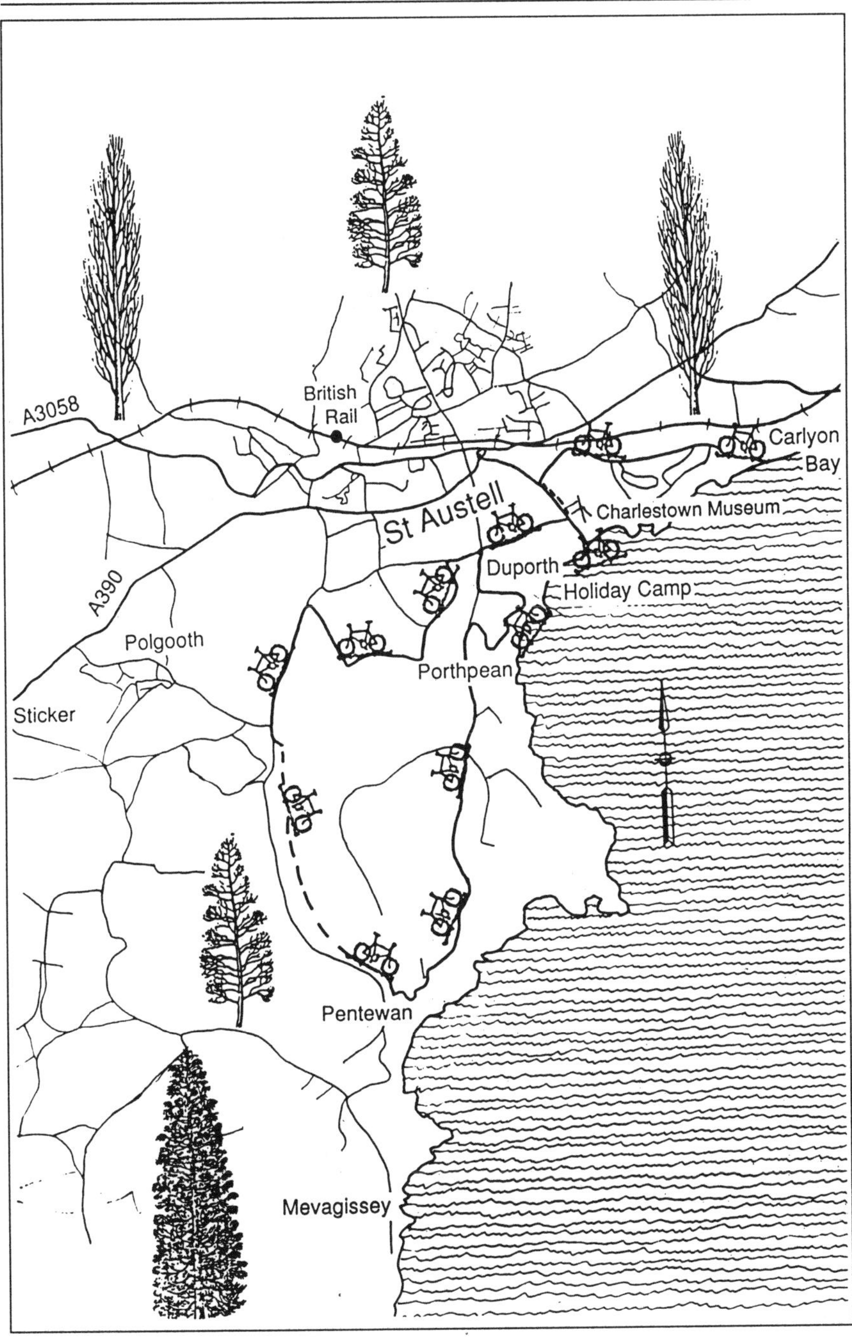
British Rail
A3058
Carlyon Bay
St Austell
Charlestown Museum
A390
Duporth
Holiday Camp
Polgooth
Porthpean
Sticker
Pentewan
Mevagissey

11. Turn right here and you will descend into Pentewan Valley adjacent to the sewage works!
12. At the road junction of the B3273, turn left and continue through the village of London Apprentice.
13. Just on the edge of this village, turn left past the concrete works and turn right alongside the stream to join the clearly marked Pentewan Cycle Trail.
14. Follow the trail which will pass through some pleasant woodland scenery and you will emerge in Pentewan Village just past a cycle hire facility.
15. Turn left through the village and follow the road past the harbour. (If you want to visit the beach here, you will need to turn right through the gate just at the end of the harbour). If not...
16. Continue out of the village and follow the road for four kilometres before the right turn to Lower Porthpean.
17. Take this turn if you want to visit the cove; the road leads back to rejoin the road that you are on. Alternatively, if your legs are tired and you want to avoid the climb out of Lower Porthpean, continue straight ahead. You will soon see the Hospice and sports ground, now on your left.
18. Turn right at the crossroads and retrace your route, through Charlestown to return to Carlyon Bay.

Nearby

The tall ships at Charlestown are all seaworthy and come and go from time to time. If you are lucky, you may see the flurry of activity as one of these magnificent vessels prepares to set sail. The vast hopper chutes above the old harbour were designed for loading china clay into the holds of ships.

St Austell is dominated by the huge conical mounds on the high ground to the north of the town. These are the heaps of the sand and quartz spoils from the china clay pits that currently form the backbone of the local economy.

Ride 8

The Camel Trail

Padstow to Bodmin Moor, North Cornwall. A Railway Path.

A superb railway path following the valley and the wide estuary of the Camel River.

Maps: Landranger 1:50,000 series. Sheet number 200.

Distance: Padstow to Wadebridge – 5½ miles (9km). Wadebridge to Bodmin – 5½ miles (9km). Bodmin to Poley's Bridge – 5½ miles (9km).

Waymarked: Yes.

Gradients: Easy, verging on non-existent.

General surface description: Crushed Stone. Smooth and well drained.

Future proposals: N/A

Other cycle routes linking: N/A

Bicycle hire: Padstow, Wadebridge and Bodmin.

Shops and refreshments: Padstow, Wadebridge, Bodmin and a few pubs/cafes signed near the trail.

Special comments: On a windy day, concentrate on the inland sections of the trail centred on Bodmin.

Special warnings: N/A

Permits: Only required for locally operated hire bikes. (Will be included in hire charge.)

The Camel Trail follows the route and the disused track bed of the Bodmin and Wadebridge Railway, which was built in the 1830s to transport sea sand inland as a soil alkali. Return trips carried granite and china clay to ships in the Camel estuary at Wadebridge. The line was abandoned after nationalisation and has only recently been updated to provide this fine public recreational pathway.

The path's surface is purpose-built for cycling, walking and movement of wheelchairs and because of its railway origins, enjoys

Family fun on the Camel Trail

level gradients and a well-drained substructure. It offers a clear 15 mile (24km) stretch of easy, traffic-free cycling, all on a tarmac or consolidated surface, where both the novice cyclist or the hardened enthusiast can capture equal pleasure. A novice rider should easily and comfortably cover the route one way in two or three hours' cycling.

The track bed runs from Poley's Bridge, on the edge of Bodmin Moor, through the outskirts of Bodmin and then, following the River Camel through the centre of Wadebridge, on to Padstow. There are many places along the route to stop and enjoy the scenery and plenty of benches for rest or picnicking use.

Access Points

Wadebridge. A good place to start, and travel in either direction. You will have no problems finding the trail.

Bodmin. A spur of the trail runs up to Bodmin. At the end of the spur, turn right to head for the moors or left and down-river for

Wadebridge and Padstow. The car park access for the trail is clearly signed from the centre of the town.

Padstow. Head up the estuary. Miles to go before you have turn back. The trail heads up-river from the back of the car park following within yards of the waterfront.

Poley's Bridge. Not much here. Easy parking and nice surroundings. From the A30, follow the signs towards Helland or Blisland. An excellent car park is situated opposite an English China Clay plant.

The Route

Throughout its whole length, the Camel Trail enjoys compacted hard surface and is excellent for cycling or walking. The barely detectable gradients make for very relaxed progress. You will not need directions. The route of the trail is clearly signed and obvious to follow.

The River Camel is virtually alongside the trail to Padstow from Poley's Bridge, flowing initially through beautiful wooded valleys before widening into a gentle sandy estuary beyond Wadebridge and flowing on to the sea at Padstow. Throughout the route there is an extraordinary and varied spectacle of bird and wildlife. There is a sense that the railway is still alive, and the careful observer will soon work out the clues to the industrial archeology of the area.

Nearby

The three towns of **Bodmin, Wadebridge** and **Padstow** are all very worthy of closer inspection. Grand granite **Bodmin** has a sense of authority and the old Gaol is worth a visit. Wadebridge was once a busy port, serviced by the railway (that is now the Camel Trail), but now it's a lovely quiet Cornish river town. Have a wander into the back streets and find a few interesting little shops. **Padstow** is the typification of a Cornish fishing town. Behind the picturesque busy harbour are a maze of narrow streets which should be explored. A ferry ride across to Rock will take you to miles of quiet beaches. Along the tranquillity of the estuary there are numerous delightful creeks.

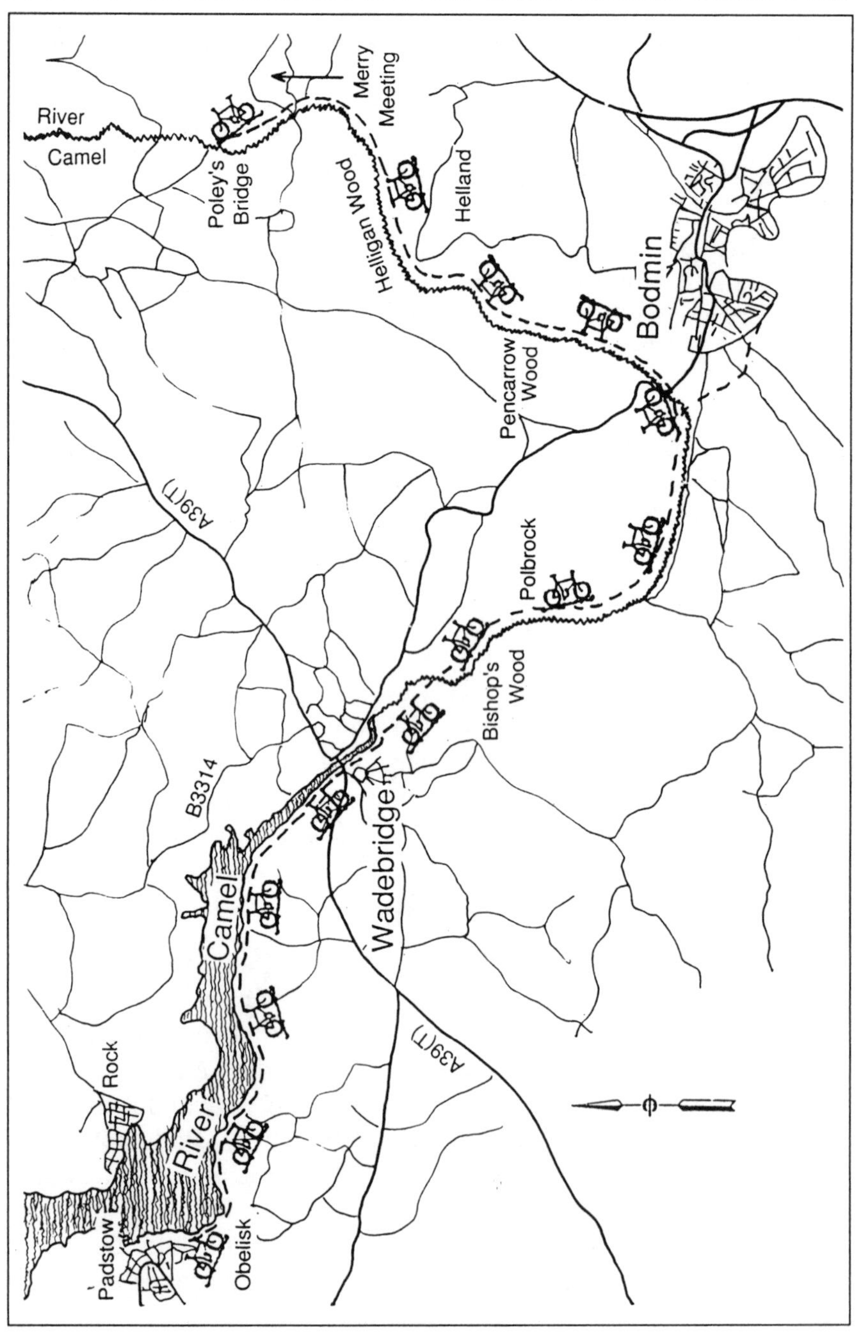
River
Camel
Poley's
Bridge
Merry
Meeting
Helligan Wood
Helland
Bodmin
Pencarrow
Wood
A39(T)
Polbrock
Bishop's
Wood
B3314
Wadebridge
Camel
River
Rock
A39(T)
Padstow
Obelisk

The history of the Bodmin and Wadebridge Railway was typical of a lot of railways created in the early 19th-century boom. Business carrying freight was steady to begin with and flourished in the 1860s with the introduction of passengers. They travelled for reasons as varied as a day by the estuary, the spectacle of a public execution on the gallows at Bodmin Gaol, or simply the need to do business or buy supplies in Bodmin. The extension to Padstow was built in 1899 and was an immediate commercial success, carrying many thousands of passengers until its closure in the 1960s. There is little doubt that the line would still be well used if it was still open to trains.

John Betjeman, who was a regular visitor to the area, described the Padstow section:

"The next five and a half miles, beside the broadening Camel to Padstow, is the most beautiful train journey I know.".

Swap the word 'train' for 'bicycle' and the same words would apply today.

Ride 9

Cardinham Woods near Bodmin, Cornwall

A safe and gentle off-road forest route. An ideal introduction to cycling for all the family.

Maps: Landranger 1:50,000 series. Sheet number 200.

Distance: Total return ride 5 miles (7.2 km).

Waymarked: Follow the cycle markers.

Gradients: Hardly at all. A couple of very short gentle gradients.

General surface description: Well-drained compacted forestry road.

Future proposals: N/A

Other cycle routes linking: None directly.

Bicycle hire: At the main car park in the woods.

Shops and refreshments: The Woodland Cafe is by the main car park in the woods.

Special comments: This is an ideal introduction to cycling for young children. For more details on the Bodmin and Wenford Steam Railway contact them at 'The General Station, Bodmin, Cornwall, PL31 1AQ.

Special warnings: N/A

Permits: N/A

This is an easy, fairly short loop ride which follows forestry roads in the valley of a natural, boulder-strewn stream. Cycle hire is available in the main car park during the warmer seasons but the ride is available throughout the year. This is an ideal location for family groups and the perfect spot to introduce newcomers to a taste of the delights of forestry cycling.

Cardinham Woods is a commercial forestry plantation extending to just over 650 acres. It was acquired by the forestry commission in 1922 and the intervening years of careful planting and replanting of mainly Douglas Fir have created a wonderfully lush forest which, as well as being a commercial success, offers a range of great leisure opportunities for cyclists, walkers, bird watchers and picnickers.

Cardinham Woods

As well as the cycling facility, there are other family enticements which include an exciting children's assault/fitness course and a nature trail, both just behind the main car park. Walkers may be tempted to climb the valley sides on one of three waymarked trails while steam train enthusiasts will be drawn the short distance to Colesloggett Halt, a station stop on the Bodmin and Wenford Steam Railway which runs the length of the Glynn Valley. The Woodland Cafe is also situated just off the main car park.

Access Points

To find Cardinham Woods from Bodmin, take the A38 towards Liskeard. 400 metres beyond Carminow Cross A30 roundabout turn left following the brown tourist signs for Cardinham Woods. Take the first left and follow the lane to the end where you will find the car park. Interpretative boards in the car park contain interesting information.

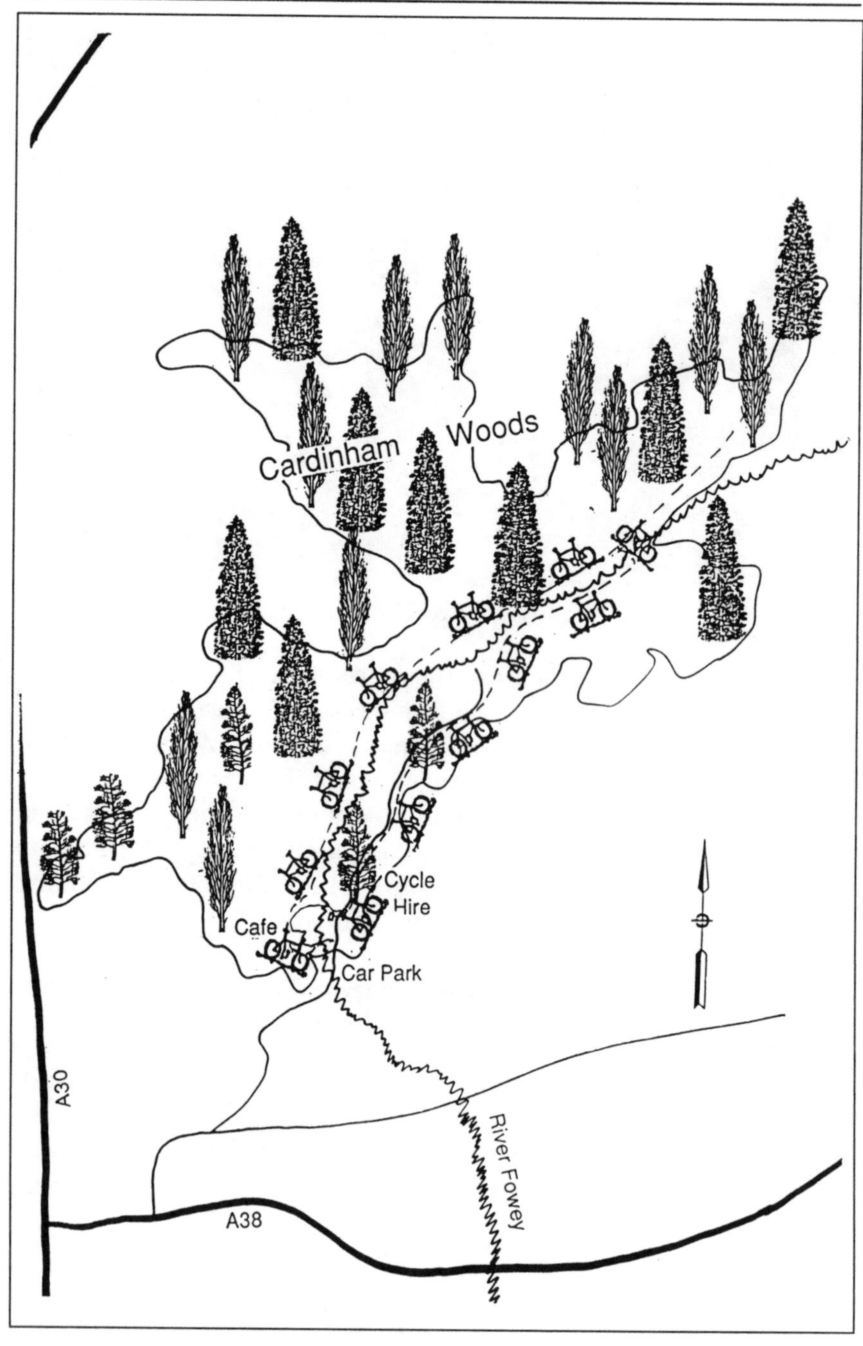
Cardinham Woods
Cycle Hire
Cafe
Car Park
A30
A38
River Fowey

The Route

1. Leave the main car park by turning left at the point where you entered from right. For a very short distance you will follow a tarmac road, which is only used occasionally by motor vehicles for access to a couple of woodland cottages. The stream will be constantly close by on your left. It is well worth stopping occasionally just to enjoy the beauty of the water and the wild flowers in the lush base of the stream valley. Keep still for long enough and you are quite lightly to see examples of squirrels and dormice who live here.
2. After about a couple of miles, you will see Vale Bridge on your left. Cross the stream here and return on the stream-side track on the other side. This is only a short ride but is very popular with local cyclists who often extend their legs by riding around the loop several times. If you want to explore further, continue up-stream or take the panoramic route on the far side of the stream.

Nearby

The nearest major town is Bodmin and the ideal way to visit from Cardinham Woods is via the Bodmin and Wenford Steam Railway. You can catch a train from Colesloggett Halt which is situated just half a mile from the car park. A timetable is posted on the platform. Bodmin was once the major town in Cornwall, a status which has now been largely lost to Truro. The once infamous Bodmin Gaol is now a nightclub/pub and museum. Another museum in the town is on the site of the former barracks of the Duke of Cornwall's Light Infantry and contains a wide selection of artifacts relating to the regiment's long and bloody history. The 144-foot obelisk, on the hill SW of the town, is a famous local landmark. It was erected in 1856 in memory of Sir Walter Raleigh Gilbert of the Indian Army.

Ride 10

Exploring Bodmin Moor, Cornwall.

A day's ride around some of the magical attractions of Bodmin Moor: St Neot, Jamaica Inn, Dozmary Pool, Golitha Falls and Colliford Lake.

Maps: Landranger 1:50,000 series. Sheet number 201.

Distance: Total return ride 17½ miles (28 km).

Waymarked: No.

Gradients: There are some climbs out of St Neot and the river valley and a few serious undulations but the rest of the ride is remarkably flat.

General surface description: Tarmac minor road.

Future proposals: N/A

Other cycle routes linking: N/A

Bicycle hire: Bodmin.

Shops and refreshments: St Neot, Bolventor.

Special comments: N/A

Special warnings: This ride is on public roads. *Be seen!*

Permits: N/A

This is a great introduction to the peaceful sleepy village of St Neot and the wild beauty of the southern part of Bodmin Moor. This is a moderately easy day-long ride or a fairly strenuous half-day ride; some of the moorland sections can be exposed on windy days so make sure you have taken the weather conditions into account before setting out. This ride is based on a suggested route by the South East Cornwall Discovery Centre's leaflet, 'Cycling in South-east Cornwall', which is designed to encourage cycle tourism in the region. It is well conceived and gives a good feel for the area.

Amongst the numerous places of interest along the route, and as well as St Neot, there are three major points of diverse interest, Colliford Lake and Dozmary Pool, Jamaica Inn and Golitha Falls.

Try to pay a visit or linger at all of them, for they each have something to offer. The lanes are generally quiet and therefore there is a minimum of contact with motor traffic, thus ensuring that it is a safe family ride.

The route passes through some delightful countryside ranging from farmland to wild moor and some sections follow heavily sheltered lanes cut into the rock. From Golitha Falls to Bolventor, the ride follows the valley of the River Fowey as it rushes down from the high moorland in the North. Archeologists will be interested in the various hut and stone circles high above the road just south east of Bolventor. There is much wild flower and wild life along the route including the possibility of seeing wild cats which are said to roam the moor.

Access Points

The ride is described with a starting point from the centre of St Neot village where there is a convenient car park. You can also start from some other point along the route. Jamaica Inn would be a good choice. The directions are anti-clockwise to avoid as many right-hand turns as possible.

The Route

1. From the car park in the centre of St Neot turn right to take the road in an easterly direction passing the church on your left.
2. Take the left fork uphill out of the village signed to Bolventor.
2. Go straight ahead at the crossroads signed Liskeard.
3. Take the narrow lane to the left shortly after the crossroads signed to Draynes and Trenant.
3. Continue straight ahead to Golitha Falls.
4. Turn left at the 'T' junction just past the Golitha Falls complex and keep on this road to Bolventor.
5. Go left onto the old A30 and then immediately left opposite Jamaica Inn to head south towards Colliford Lake and Dozmary Pool (signed Dozmary Pool and St Neot).

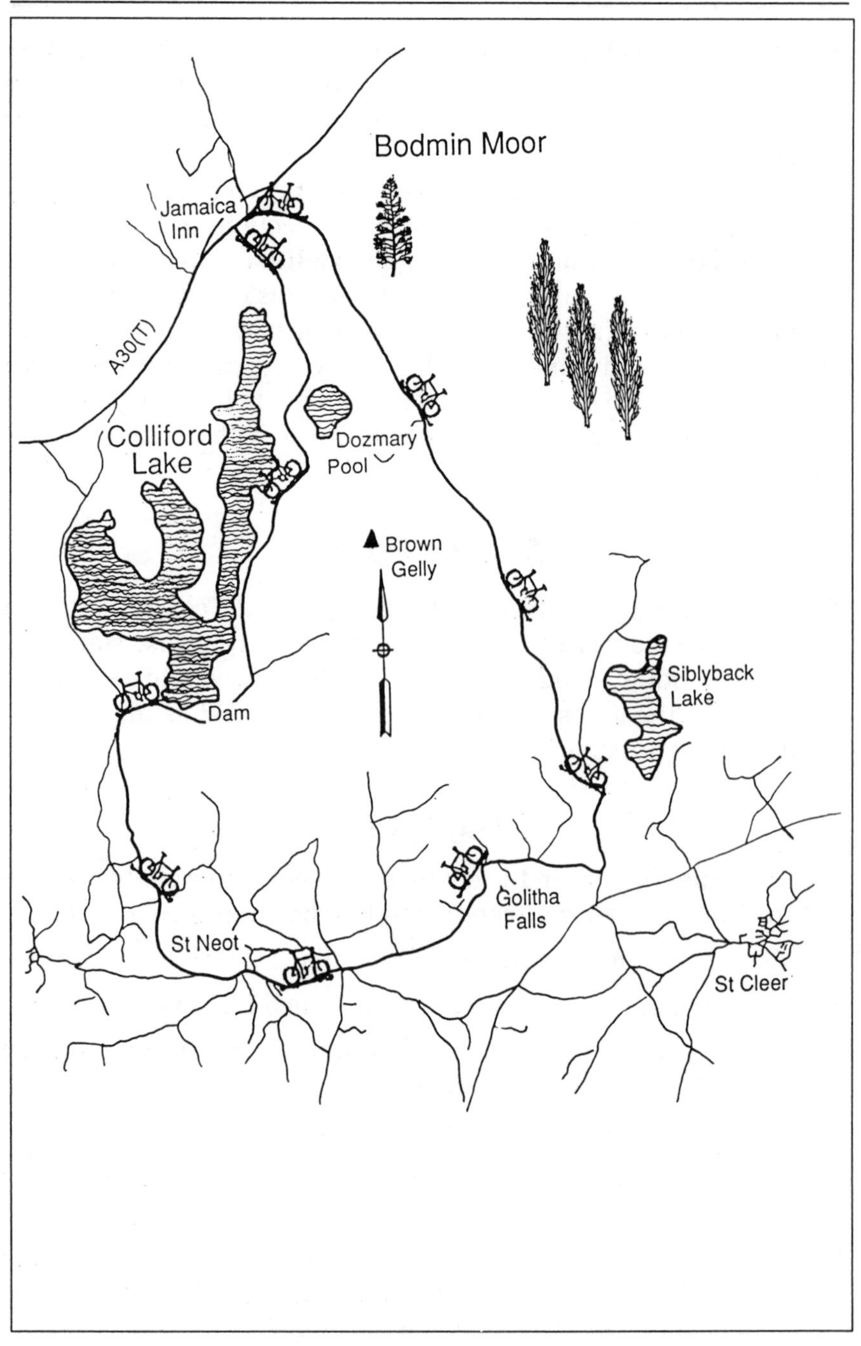
Bodmin Moor
Jamaica Inn
A30(T)
Colliford Lake
Dozmary Pool
Brown Gelly
Siblyback Lake
Dam
Golitha Falls
St Neot
St Cleer

6. Continue straight ahead, Dozmary Pool on your left and the great expanse of Colliford Lake on your right.
7. Ignore the first turn to St Neot and continue to go right below the face of the dam.
8. Turn left at the next 'T' junction signed St Neot.
9. Continue straight ahead over the cattle grid onto the unfenced road on Letter Moor.
10. Continue along this road before turning to return to St Neot.

Nearby

Dozmary Pool is considered in Cornish folklore to have supernatural and magic properties. There is no obvious feeder stream and this combines with the unusual crystal clarity of the water and its lonely moorland location to create a mysterious atmosphere.

The Tregeagle is a Cornish ghost who is supposed to have sold his soul to the Devil in order to marry a rich heiress. His allotted payment to the Devil was to bail out Dozmary Pool with a leaky

Jamaica Inn, Bodmin Moor

limpet shell – hence the local expression 'to bale out Dozmary Pool with a limpet shell' meaning to do the impossible.

Daphne Du Maurier's book 'Jamaica Inn' turned this lonely moorland inn into a popular tourist attraction. The commercial advantage of the establishment is heavily exploited and the ping of microwave ovens has replaced the popular conception of the wood burning range.

The pair of standing stones east of Golitha Falls, known as 'King Doniert's Stone', are noted for the geometric patterns and the Latin inscription to the Cornish king who drowned nearby in 875 AD. Golitha Falls are a spectacular sight and very much worth a visit.

Ride 11

Looe Valley Route and Kilminorth Woods, Cornwall

A superb day's ride, up the East Looe River valley from Looe to Liskeard and returning to Looe down the West Looe River valley and through Kilminorth Woods.

Maps: Landranger 1:50,000 series. Sheet number 201.

Distance: Total return ride 23½ miles (35 km).

Waymarked: No.

Gradients: Some short steep climbs and a lot of sweeping descents. Mainly downhill on the return to Looe interspersed with a few climbs.

General surface description: Tarmac.

Future proposals: N/A

Other cycle routes linking: N/A

Bicycle hire: Looe.

Shops and refreshments: The main centres are Looe and Liskeard. This is a very pleasant full day's ride and Liskeard will be perfectly placed for lunch. There are also facilities in Causeland, Trewidland and Herodsfoot.

Special comments: N/A

Special warnings: The main A387 road out of Looe, which is used for the first short section of the route, is either busy or very busy in summer. At least it is not too far and the rest of the route utilises very quiet lanes.

Permits: N/A

This is a delightful full day's ride based on the seaside resort of Looe and the two Looe Rivers which confluence just north of the town. The first part of the ride climbs gently uphill from the coast, broadly following the course of the Looe Valley Railway. Unfortunately the first 3 km are on the main A 387, an unavoidable exercise to access the network of beautiful quiet country lanes that make up the rest of the ride. You will pass through a series of lovely, unspoilt, mainly riverside villages before reaching Liskeard which offers plenty of interest to the urban explorer. The second part of the ride follows the lushly wooded West Looe river valley back to Looe, taking you through more delightful hamlets and villages before leading you to the last few kilometres into Looe, through the magnificent beauty of Kilminorth Wood. This ride is very loosely based on a suggested route by the South East Cornwall Discovery Centre's leaflet, 'Cycling in Southeast Cornwall', which is designed to encourage cycle tourism in the region. It is well conceived and gives a good feel for the area.

Looe describes a town in two parts plus an island. East Looe and West Looe are joined by a seven-arched Victorian bridge just below the confluence of the East and West Looe Rivers while Looe Island, which is noted for the remains of an old monastery and is in private ownership, lies just off shore south of Hannafore point. Only a few yards of water separate Looe Island from the mainland at low tide. During World War II, Looe island was bombed by an German aircraft whose pilot mistook it for a battleship. West Looe is notable for its hotels which offer accommodation for thousands of visitors throughout the year. East Looe is a most charming fishing town with

Waterside in Kilminorth Woods

a delightful maze of old cobbled streets. The 13th-century tower of St Mary's Church is white-painted to act as a day mark for sailors and the 16th-century Old Guildhall houses a museum of local artifacts.

Liskeard was a chartered Stannary town which, until the late 19th century, drew great wealth from the very prosperous Caradon Hill Copper Mine. It is now more noted for its very busy livestock market which serves the local rural community. Liskeard is on the main Penzance to London railway route and is also the terminus for the adorable Looe branch line.

Access Points

The route is based on Looe and the directions are given from Looe Station. There is limited car parking here but there are plenty of other car parks in and around Looe; in the height of summer it is a matter of finding one with a space. The best car park is by the discovery centre.

The Route

1. If you arrive by car, when you have parked somewhere in or around Looe make your way to Looe Station on the A387 just outside the town. This is clearly signed. Do not try to park at the station itself as the facility is very restricted.
2. Turn left out of the car park and, with care, proceed north along the A387 for 3 kilometres.
3. Fork left onto the B3254 in the village of Sandplace, signed to Duloe.
4. After ½ a kilometre fork right along a minor road which follows the line of the railway on your left, crossing to right after a short distance.
5. Continue along this road for 2 kilometres before turning right to cross the railway just past Causeland Station (signed Trewidland).
6. A short steep climb will take you to Trewidland.

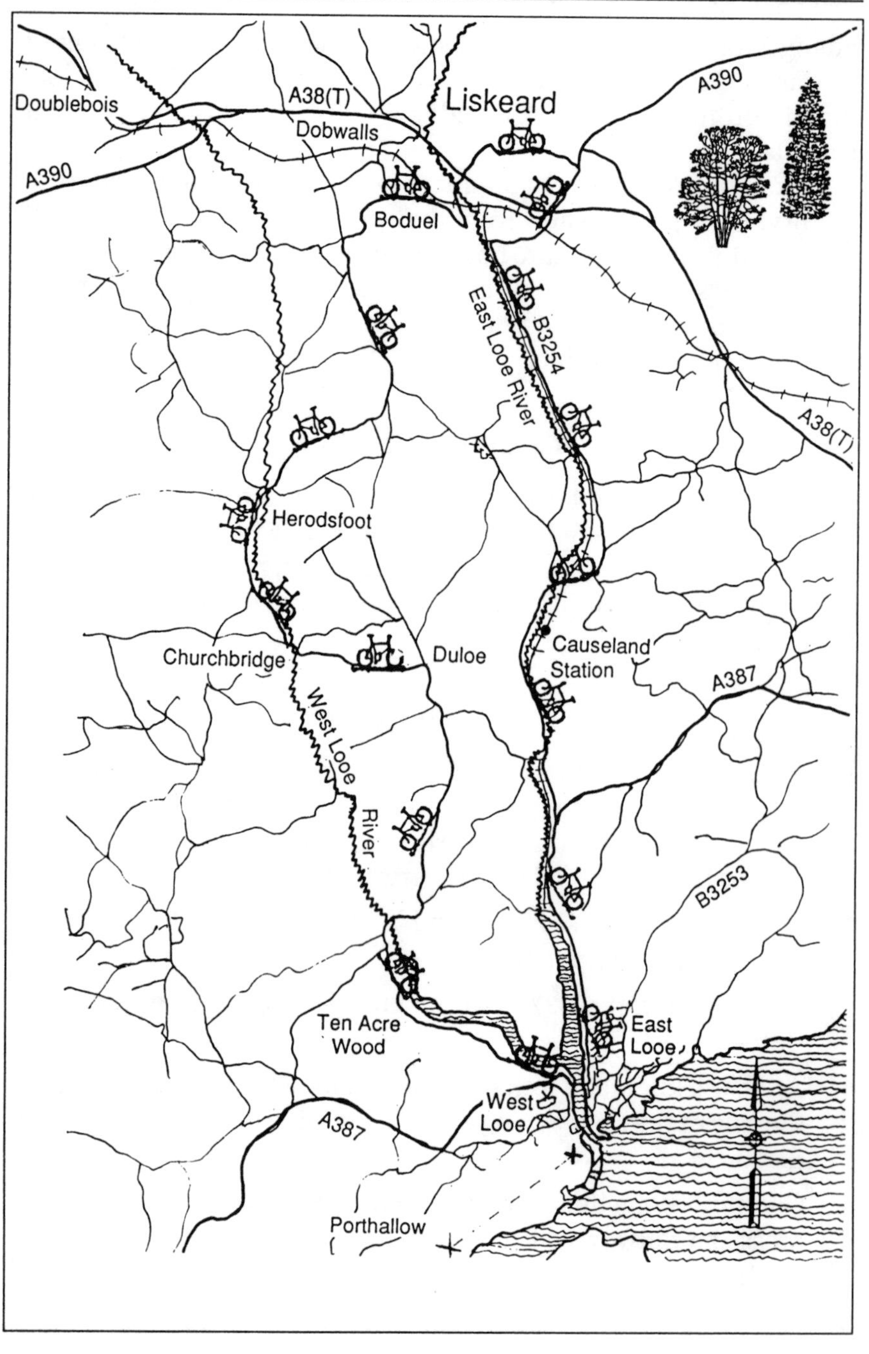
Doublebois
A38(T)
Liskeard
A390
Dobwalls
A390
Boduel
East Looe River
B3254
A38(T)
Herodsfoot
Churchbridge
Duloe
Causeland
Station
A387
West Looe
River
B3253
Ten Acre
Wood
East
Looe
West
Looe
A387
Porthallow

7. Continue left at the 'T' junction and left again at the phone box in the village centre (signed Trewidland School).
8. A short descent will take you back towards the railway which will be on your left.
9. A fork, once again staying close to the railway, which will still be on your left.
10. At the 'T' junction with the B3254 turn left towards Liskeard then continue north for another kilometre.
11. Where the B3254 starts to climb, turn left again along the single track road and continue ahead, keeping the railway on your left.
12. In Coombe, after bearing right, turn sharp right and rejoin the B3254 by turning left. Follow this road over the railway and the A38 into Liskeard.
13. Explore Liskeard.
14. By the war memorial in Liskeard, facing the Fountain Hotel, head out of town via West Street and Old Road, passing Liskeard School.
15. Follow Old Road to the right. After passing under the A38, you will reach a 'T' junction, take the left turn for Looe.
16. Pass under the railway viaduct and take the sharp uphill right.
17. At the junction bear left into the No Through Road and carry straight on into the unmade track.
18. Turn right at the 'T' junction.
19. Turn left at the cross roads and continue straight ahead.
20. Take the third right at the top of the rise in the road.
21. After a sharp descent, turn right in Herodsfoot.
22. Keep left out of the village, keeping the river and the war memorial on your left.
23. Descend through the wooded valley and, after crossing a small brook, take the bridleway on your left which will follow the river bank to Churchbridge.
24. At Churchbridge, turn left over the bridge and uphill to Duloe.

25. In Duloe turn right along the B3254 for ½ kilometre (signed Looe).
26. When the road bends sharply to the left, carry straight ahead along the minor road.
27. At the 5-way junction of roads and tracks, after about 2 kilometres, turn right and descend to the West Looe River (signed Pelynt, Polperro).
28. At the bottom of a steep descent, cross the river and follow around to the left.
29. Keep left again after a short distance and left again (signed Kilminorth and Watergate).
30. At Watergate village, ignore the public footpath along the river and carry on a little further up the hill to a point where you will see a stone retaining wall on your left. Take the bridleway to the left here signed Looe.
30. Follow the woodland trail back to Looe. There are some lovely views as well as wild flowers and a rich variety of wild creatures scurrying in and out of the tree cover. Do not forget to stop and enjoy.

Nearby

The South East Cornwall Discovery Centre, just to the north of the main centre of Looe, offers a free exhibition and video presentation which will give you an insight into the history, culture and magical beauty of the region.

Ride 12

A Ride Around Roadford Lake, West Devon.

Around Roadford Lake via quiet country lanes and sleepy villages with some optional excursions to the lake shore.

Maps: Landranger 1:50,000 series. Sheet number 190.

Distance: Total return ride 16 miles (26 km).

Waymarked: No.

Gradients: A few ups and downs as the ground rises away from the lake shore.

General surface description: Tarmac public roads.

Future proposals: N/A

Other cycle routes linking: N/A

Bicycle hire: Okehampton.

Shops and refreshments: Roadford Lake Dam – main car park / visitor centre. Germansweek village.

Special comments: N/A

Special warnings: N/A

Permits: N/A

This is a ride around the very quiet traditional Devon country lanes away from the main coastal and moorland tourist centres. Based on Roadford Lake, the route takes you in a wide circle and passes through a couple of sleepy villages along the way. At various points you have the option of making short detours from the main route down virtually forgotten no-through-roads to the shores of the lake.

Roadford Lake is one Britain's newest reservoirs. It was completed in October 1989 and was built to help cope with the extra demands imposed on Devon's water supply during the height of the tourist season, a time which coincides with the driest and therefore highest drought-risk period. South West Water describe Roadford Lake as giant holding tank. By using rivers and an underground pipe network, water can be distributed to a range of destinations more or less by turning the correct sequence of valves. Centres of population which may draw on Roadford's water include Torbay and Plymouth via the natural rivers and North Cornwall and North Devon via the pipe network.

This part of Devon is well away from the tourist spots of Dartmoor and the coastal regions. The A30 trunk road, only a few short miles to the south, carries an endless stream of traffic in and out of the south west peninsula and few people venture into the Roadford area purely for the pleasure of a visit. Their loss is your gain, as the area provides some of the finest parts of unspoilt Devon.

Access Points

The start and finish of the ride is at the Roadford Lake main car park on the eastern end of the dam. Teas, coffees, sandwiches and light lunches are available at the tea rooms adjacent to the car park. From Okehampton, head west on the A30. After about 8 miles you will take the minor roads to the north for Roadford Lake and Bratton Clovelly. The lake is well signed from all of the surrounding main roads and villages and the sign-posting will direct you to the dam and the main car park.

A shady resting place

The Route

1. From the main pay and display car park, turn left away from the dam.
2. After half a mile, turn left, to Bratton Clovelly. After half a mile, for an optional lakeside excursion, turn left down the road marked 'Road Closed' and ride 800 metres to the lakeside. To continue, go straight ahead for another half mile before turning left signed 'Germansweek'.
3. After half a mile, you can reach the lake on foot from the roadside anglers' car park. To continue, after a mile you will come to a graceful modern bridge across the northern end of the lake.
4. A quarter of a mile beyond the bridge, another route to the lake turns left down the lane signed Toft. A 1000 metre ride will see you at the lakeside. To continue, go straight ahead for half a mile and then turn right into Germansweek village.
5. Continue straight through Germansweek and for another half mile to Eworth village.
6. Turn left here opposite the phone box.
7. After another quarter of a mile go left again.
8. After half a mile go straight on at the crossroads signed Ashwater.
9. After passing through Witherdon Wood, the road will climb up to a 'T' junction.
10. Turn left here, to Roadford Lake and Ashwater.
11. Turn left at the staggered 'schoolhouse crossroads' signed Roadford Lake and Broadwood.
12. Continue straight ahead and after one mile turn left to Grinacombe Cross.
13. After a short distance you will see a magnificent view of Roadford Lake and Dam. At the crossroads ahead turn right (signed Roadford Lake) to continue the route (an optional lakeside excursion 400 metres to lakeside straight ahead).
14. Turn left at the 'T' junction and continue straight ahead for one

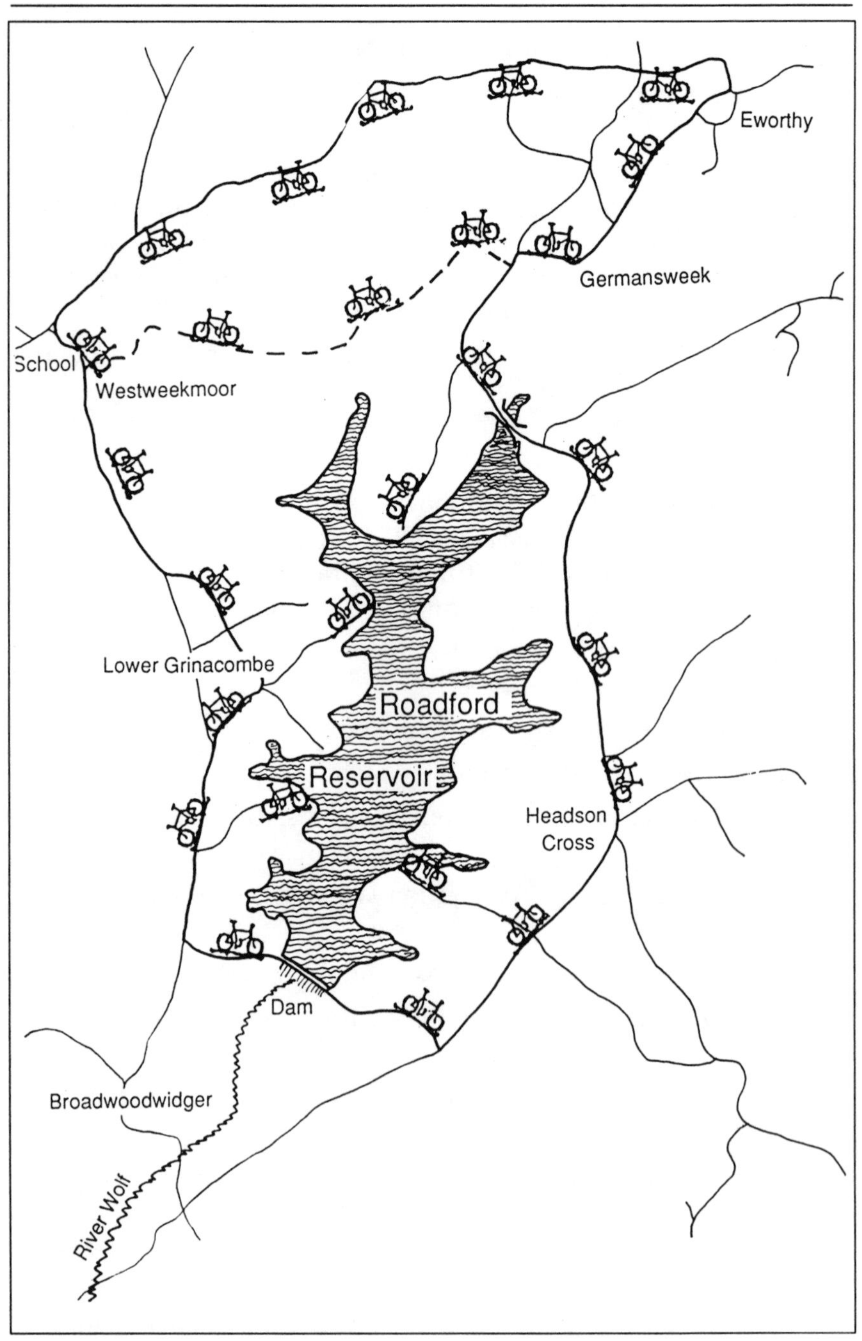
Eworthy
Germansweek
School
Westweekmoor
Lower Grinacombe
Roadford
Reservoir
Headson
Cross
Dam
Broadwoodwidger
River Wolf

mile, following around to the right to return to the original car park. (Just before arriving at the dam, a left turn will take you lakeside to the water sports centre where fishing permits are available.)

A Short Cut: Just before a right turn to Germansweek (4), on the left is a bridleway. If you wish to shorten the ride by approx three miles, take this bridleway and follow it for just over a mile. When you rejoin the tarmac lane, turn left and you will be just beyond the 'school house crossroads' (11) at Westweekmoor. This stony bridleway is muddy, and slippery when wet.

Nearby

As the ride is centred on Roadford Lake, here are some interesting data: Lake completed October 1989; water capacity 8,350 million litres; water surface area 730 acres; deepest point 120 feet; length of dam 1,411 feet; height of dam 133 feet; length of lake 2.6 miles; main feeder River Wolf; wintering wildfowl 2,000 in 1994 and increasing; number of trees planted – 150,000; evidence of human occupation – 5,000 years.

There is an extremely wide range of wild flora in the area and a walk along the lakeside is very much recommended.

Ride 13

The Tarka Trail Braunton to Petrockstowe, North Devon.

A riverside railway path to the coast passing through glorious valley and estuary scenery.

Maps: Landranger 1:50,000 series. Sheet numbers 180 and 191.

Distance: Total return ride: Braunton to Petrockstowe 30 miles (48 km).

Waymarked: Yes. Clear waymarks throughout the route.

Gradients: Virtually flat.

General surface description: Well-drained consolidated stone and gravel railway trackbed. Purpose built for cycling.

Future proposals: N/A

Other cycle routes linking: Maybe one day soon? (See special comments and Ride 28).

Bicycle hire: Hirers in Barnstaple, Braunton, Yelland, Bideford, and Great Torrington.

Shops and refreshments: Plenty of places along the route. Good concentrations in Bideford and Barnstaple. Good facilities at Petrockstowe (signed) by taking to the road and making a short climb beyond the end of the trail.

Special comments: There is currently a firm proposal to extend the route northwards to Ilfracombe. (Ride 28).

Special warnings: N/A

Permits: N/A

The Tarka Trail, in its totality, is a 180-mile footpath around the North Devon area, named after the otter in Henry Williamson's 1927 award-winning novel. 150 miles of the Tarka Trail imposes a strict no-cycling policy but this is very well compensated for by the remaining 30 miles of trail which is specified as a joint trail for walkers and cycles. This runs along the track bed of the former Barnstaple to Meeth railway line and is undoubtedly one of the best cycling facilities in Great Britain.

Beginning at Braunton, on the north of the Taw estuary, the trail follows the water's edge to Barnstaple. From here it turns back down the south of the same estuary before cutting across to the eastern shore of the Torridge estuary and turning south to Bideford. The trail then tracks inland up the Torridge valley through cuttings, over grand bridges and through tunnels to Great Torrington and Petrockstowe, not far away from the original terminus at Meeth.

This virtually flat trail enjoys solid, smooth and well-drained surfaces. The ride is varied and interesting in both wildlife and industrial archeological senses. The Tarka Trail offers the complete ingredients for pleasurable traffic-free cycling, all set in the magnificence of some of the most beautiful river valleys and estuaries of this scenic north Devon area.

The Tarka Trail, near Petrockstowe

There is plenty to see and experience along the way. Seaside, boats, sunbathing, disused stations, jellied eels, bridges, weirs, salmon leaps, pubs, museums and shops are just the beginning of the list. There is always a new view around the next bend.

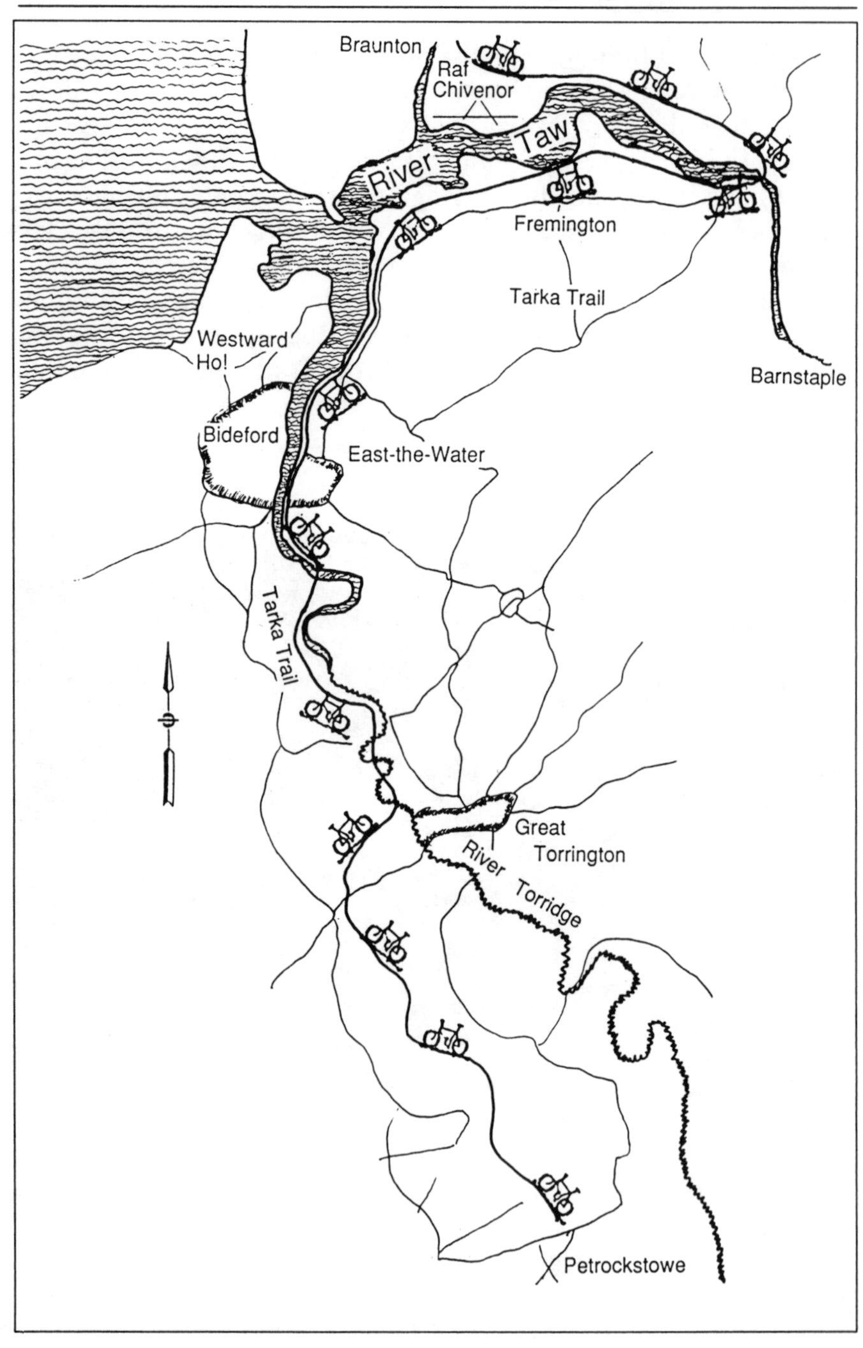
Braunton
Raf Chivenor
River Taw
Fremington
Tarka Trail
Westward Ho!
Barnstaple
Bideford
East-the-Water
Tarka Trail
Great Torrington
River Torridge
Petrockstowe

Access Points

There are plenty of good access points throughout the route. The following list is not complete but it will offer suggestions to cover the route: Braunton, West Ashford, Ashford, Barnstaple, Sticklepath, Bicklington, Fremington, Instow, Yelland, Bideford, Weare Giffard, Great Torrington, Petrockstowe.

The Route

The whole route is well waymarked and very easy to follow. You will not need detailed directions.

1. The first part of the route, from Velator Bridge in Braunton, follows the north shore of the Taw Estuary. The two estuaries along the route can have very different characters in different tidal conditions. You are guided past Chivenor and onto Barnstaple. **It is proposed to extend the route northwards to Ilfracombe.**
2. Leave Barnstaple over the Long Bridge and follow the waymarks to the trail which resumes along the southern shore of the Taw estuary passing Bicklington, Fremington and Yelland on the way to Instow. There is a good beach here. Beyond Instow, the trail is following the eastern shore of the Torridge estuary, in a southerly direction.
3. Go right over the bridge at East -the-Water into 'Bideford' and after exploring the town, continue along the trail, which again is very clearly waymarked, in a southerly direction on the east bank of the River Torridge.
4. From here the trail criss-crosses the river, passes through tunnels and gently climbs up the river valley. Cross the road and continue beyond Great Torrington to Petrockstowe, from which point the trail is for walkers only.

Nearby

Tarka was an otter born from the imagination of Henry Williamson. It is unlikely that either Tarka or his creator could predict the possibility of a cycling and walking trail being named him. By using the name, the creators of the initiative have cleverly encompassed and harnessed the vastness of his descriptive power, to the benefit of their local tourist industry.

The disused railway line forms the perfect route for a cycle trail and has been brought back to life with all the appropriate equipment necessary to create a first-class, safe, traffic-free family cycling facility.

Chivenor airfield is often busy with military aircraft movement. For aircraft spotters, there is a good viewing area on the trail just north of the airfield.

The towns of Barnstaple, Bideford and Great Torrington all have tourist information centres which will supply local town guides. They are all interesting towns worthy of exploration.

Ride 14

Lynton to Woody Bay (via the Valley of Rocks), North Devon.

An energetic ride in stunningly beautiful coastal and cliff surroundings.

Maps: Landranger 1:50,000 series. Sheet number 180.

Distance: Total return ride 10 miles (16 km).

Waymarked: No.

Gradients: Yes. Be prepared to cycle up a few hills, nothing too serious. Make the best of the views and the refreshing descents.

General surface description: Tarmac.

Future proposals: N/A

Other cycle routes linking: N/A

Bicycle hire: Lynton.

Shops and refreshments: Lynton and Woody Bay.

Special comments: Do not be too intimidated by the steep climbs. They will lead to some fantastic views and some breathtaking descents. If you take your time and pace yourself, the ride need not be too strenuous.

Special warnings: Check your brakes!

Permits: N/A Part of the route is via a toll road but there is no charge for bicycles.

This is an exciting coastal ride from Lynton to Woody Bay and the Valley of Rocks. There are some climbs and a particularly steep descent which will take your breath away. Situated in wild and beautiful countryside on the edge of Exmoor, Lynton has its modern roots firmly in the Victorian era, when it became a popular resort. It perches on top of a rocky headland well above the sea and is approached from Lynmouth via a cliff railway.

The Valley of Rocks is dominated by the imposing jagged pinnacles of eroded granite which are known by fantastic names such as 'Ragged Jack' or 'The Devil's Cheesewring'. 'Mother Meldrum's Cave'

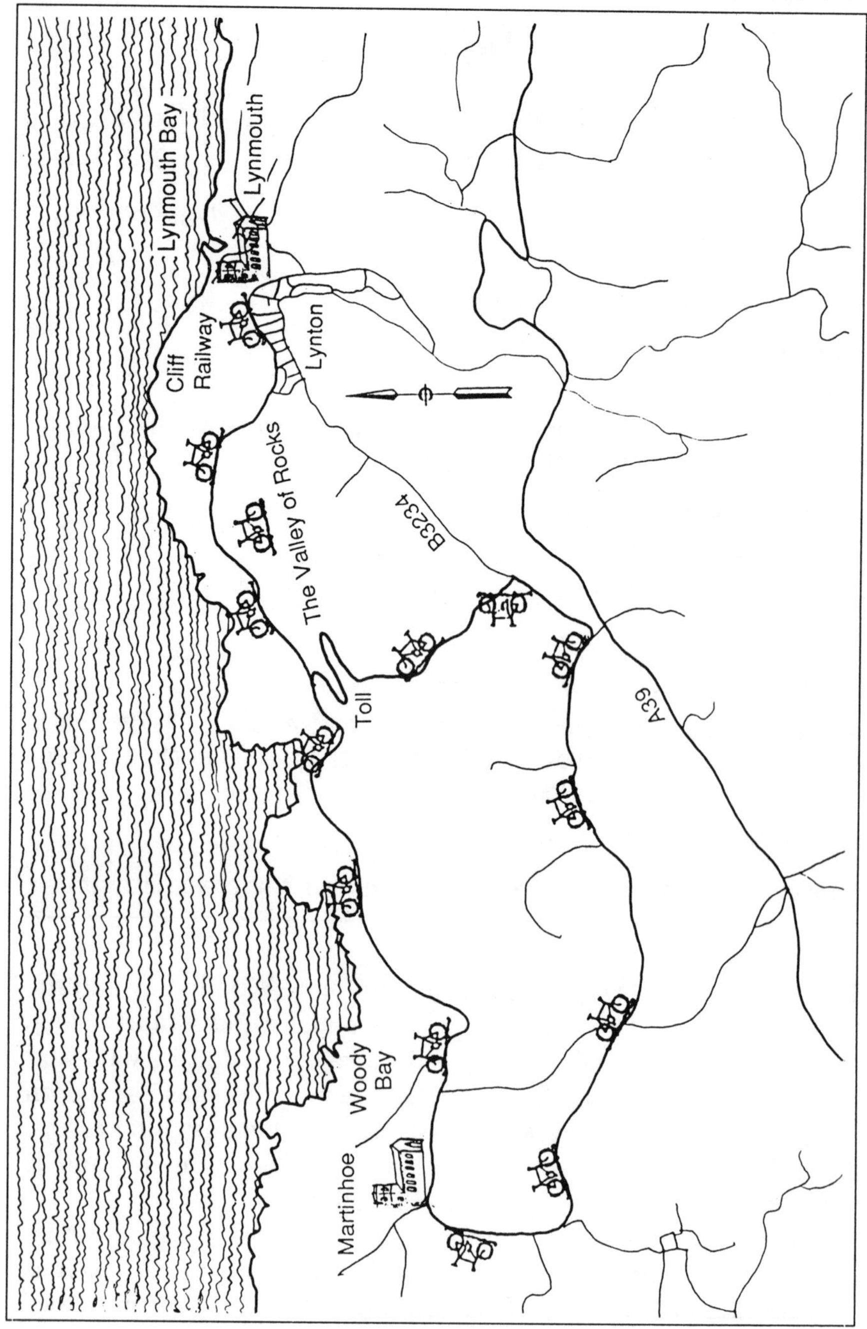
Lynmouth Bay
Lynmouth
Cliff Railway
Lynton
The Valley of Rocks
B3234
Toll
A39
Woody Bay
Martinhoe

is named after the odd witch-like woman who lived in the valley in the late 19th century. The walk/climb down to Woody Bay is an excellent chance to see the vast variety of sea birds who have set up their homes on the cliff; to name a few – auks, guillemots, kittiwakes, fulmars, shags and razorbills. The rocky cliffs here are softened by the many oak trees and rich green rhododendrons which give the bay its name.

The route follows the coast up to Woody Bay and then bends inland and climbs before returning to the Valley of Rocks. There are some magnificent views from this inland stretch. If you are feeling the slightest bit poetic, you are in the right spot. Poets who have drawn inspiration here include Wordsworth, Coleridge, Southey and Shelley who eloped here with the 16-year-old Mary Wollstonecraft, much to the annoyance of Mr and Mrs Wollstonecraft.

Access Points

The starting point of the ride is from the Tourist Information Centre in Lynton. The directions are anti-clockwise to avoid as many right-hand turns as possible. The toll road offers free access to cyclists.

The Route

1. From the tourist information centre in Lynton, leave the town to the west via the Valley of the Rocks coast road. With your back to the Lynton and Lynmouth town hall and tourist information office, turn right and leave the town with the guest houses on your right.
2. Follow the toll road and the signs for Woody Bay. Pass the Christian centre and continue up the woody coast road beyond the Valley of Rocks.
3. Above Woody Bay, take the left fork uphill. The road bends around inland to the left.
4. After climbing away from Woody Bay, at the 'T' junction go right, signposted towards Martinhoe, Hunters Inn and Parracombe.

Sign post to Mother Meldrum's Cave

5. Continue at the next junction straight ahead to Martinhoe and Hunters Inn. Continue past the 11th century St Martin's Church at Martinhoe where the road bends left.

6. Just beyond the phone box, turn left towards Parracombe, Lynton and Lynmouth.

7. At the crossroads, go left, signposted for Woody Bay and Martinhoe.

8. At the next junction, go right and retrace the route to Lynton through the Valley of Rocks.

Nearby

Exmoor is one of the most beautiful of the great National Parks and is made of a variety of landscapes varying from the rugged coastal area where this ride is based, to soft rich pasture and wild country, further inland. The most famous literary work inspired by the moor is 'Lorna Doon', by Blackmore. The villages of the moor are worth visiting; some of the more famous are Dunster, with its wide main street and 17th-century eight-sided Yarn Market building, and Parracombe with its lovely stone cottages.

Ride 15

Eggesford Forest, Mid Devon

Maps: Landranger 1:50,000 series. Sheet numbers 180 and 191.

Distance: Total available forest ride approx 4 miles (6 km).

Waymarked: Yes. Latest information and maps available at Eggesford Country Centre.

Gradients: Nothing too serious.

General surface description: Well-drained and solid forestry and minor roads.

Future proposals: N/A

Other cycle routes linking: N/A

Bicycle hire: On site at Eggesford Country Centre.

Shops and refreshments: Eggesford Country Centre.

Special comments: N/A

Special warnings: If you decide to try the rough mountain biking tracks, make sure you wear a helmet and expect a few falls.

Permits: N/A

Although the routes are short, the forest provides good traffic free family rides or, in a different part of the forest, a good section of rough riding for the dedicated mountain biker. Originally part of Eggesford Hall Estate, owned by Lord Portsmouth's wealthy family, Eggesford Forest was acquired by the Forestry Commission in 1919. Set in the backwater splendour of mid Devon and served by regular trains from the tiny Eggesford Station, the forest is is an idyllic spot with beautiful mature trees, bubbling watercourses and a fantastic array of wild flower and plant life. Reached by car on the A377 19 miles south of Barnstaple, the forest is now well into its second rotation and boasts a great variety of tree species including large areas of mature broad-leaved woodland.

The dominant trees within Eggesford are tall douglas fir, which can reach heights of over 130 feet (39½ metres), hardy european larch, elegant Norway spruce (real Christmas trees, but most are far

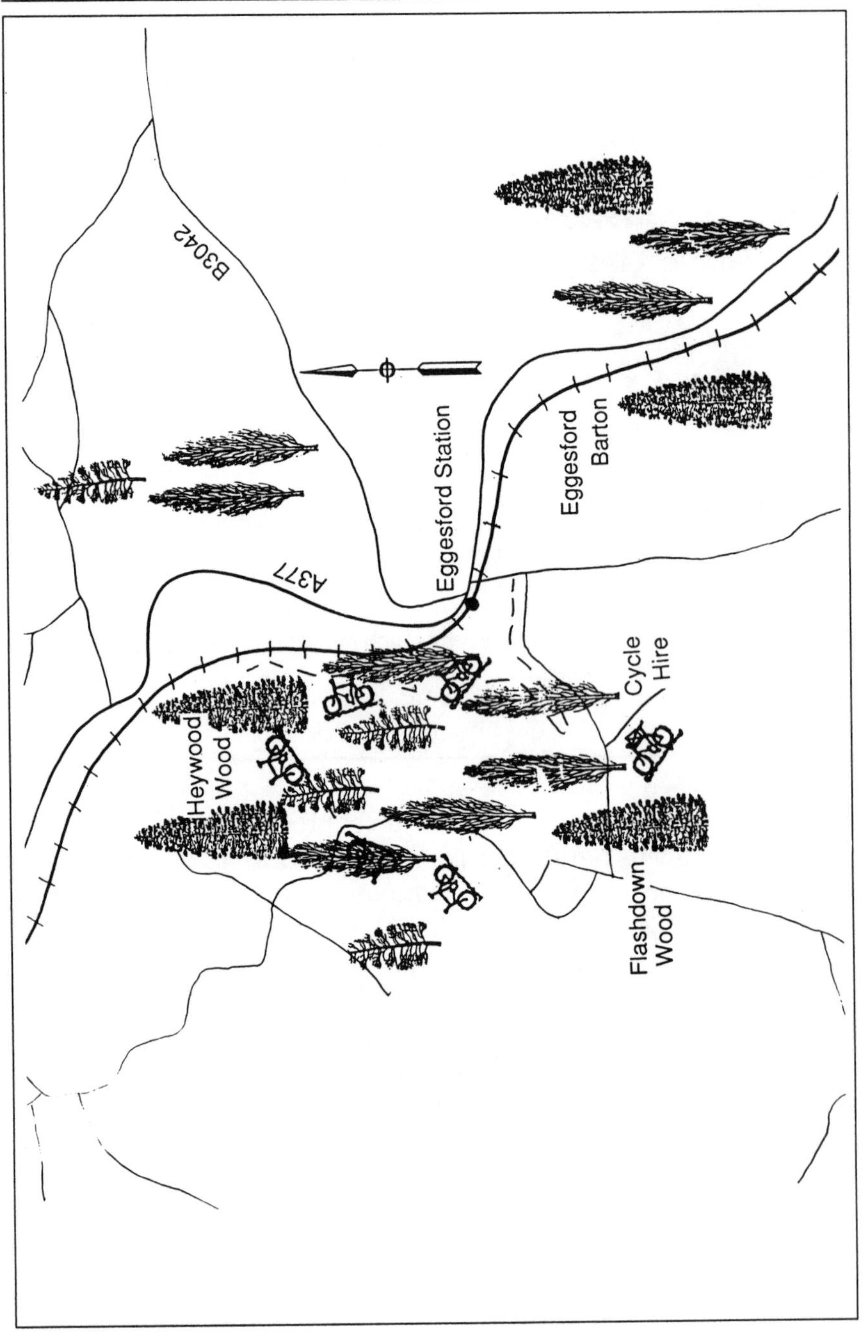
B3042
A377
Eggesford Station
Eggesford Barton
Cycle Hire
Heywood Wood
Flashdown Wood

too big for your hallway. Other species include ash and cypress while some examples of birch and oak are making ground in the clearings. Around parts of the perimeter are mature oak, ash and hawthorn which generally pre-date the managed forest.

The bird life of the forest includes heron, kingfisher, and dippers around the River Taw as well as chiff-chaff, tree creepers and wood pigeons in the woods. As well as the waymarked cycle routes, there are a range of lovely waymarked walks and a free-to-enter visitor centre with masses of information and interpretation of the forest and the Eggesford area.

Access Points

Eggesford Country Centre is situated off the A377 Exeter to Barnstaple road. One of the best ways to get to Eggesford is by train either from Barnstaple or from Exeter.

The Route

From Eggesford Country Centre there are trails leading through the forest in various directions. A very pleasant and easy route is marked You will never be far from the River Taw and its little tributaries. It forms a narrow vale through the heart of the forest and it is a delight to see the crystal clear water flowing confidently across the rock strewn stream bed. Have a rest on one of the lovely mossy shaded banks and look up through the tree canopy whilst you listen to the constant babbling of the water.

Along your chosen route, look out for birds, wild life and the masses of wild flowers in the undergrowth and hedges. In springtime primroses and violets will be in bloom while later on in the year, foxgloves and campions will provide plentiful colour. Follow the waymarks and you will come back to where you started. See how you feel and perhaps go out and do it again.

The main family route runs through Flashdown Woods and Heywood Wood. The rough mountain biking area is in Hilltown Wood.

Eggesford Forest

Nearby

Eggesford Forest is served by regular trains on the 'Tarka' Exeter to Barnstaple line. Although it is only a very small station and serves no major centre of population, the landowner whose property was acquired by the railway company only allowed the line to run through his estate on the condition that all trains must stop at Eggesford Station. This covenant is still in force today and the current train operators could well find themselves in court if they ignored it.

Ride 16

Abbeyford Woods, North of Okehampton, West Devon.

An extremely pleasant short waymarked ride through the forest, ideal for timed fitness exercises or for a short introductory family ride away from traffic.

Maps: Landranger 1:50,000 series. Sheet numbers 191.

Distance: Total return loop ride 2 miles (3.2 km).

Waymarked: Yes, follow the white markers.

Gradients: Enough to make life interesting, but quite manageable.

General surface description: Well-drained consolidated forestry track.

Future proposals: N/A

Other cycle routes linking: Ride 18, 'The West Devon Sticklepath Cycle Route', passes through Abbeyford Woods on the minor road.

Bicycle hire: Okehampton.

Shops and refreshments: Okehampton.

Special comments: N/A

Special warnings: Some fast descents. Wear a helmet.

Permits: N/A

This delightful waymarked route will take you through a wonderful diversity of forest ranging from lush glades of broadleaf trees to nursery plantations of freshly planted conifers, all within a short distance from a convenient forest car park. This is a short ride, ideal for introducing youngsters to the joys of cycling in the forest.

For fitness purposes, the route offers enough gradient to be suitable for personal training by riding against your own time targets. To make the best out of time training, set yourself an easy benchmark time by riding the route once at a normal, fairly leisurely pace. Try to improve your time by a small margin on each subsequent run. Do not make the mistake of setting out at a blistering pace and subsequently attempting to better your lap. This will do little for long-term fitness and muscular strain can put your short-term fitness in jeopardy.

Abbeyford Woods

There are some good natural wildlife observation hides in the eastern part of the wood; among the broadleaf trees and in the car park are picnic tables and interpretive boards offering a great deal of most informative detail on the local woodland habitat as well as other waymarked nature foot trails. Within the wood is a large population of grey squirrel and a smaller, but significant population of roe deer. The deer can often be closer than you think; they will always stand still when they hear you, usually behind scrub cover. To find your deer, look carefully for horizontal lines and twitching ears. Also in the eastern sector of the wood, part of the Tarka Trail leads down to the River Okement valley and onto Okehampton. A very pleasant short tarmac path, accessed from the car park, is suitable for wheelchairs.

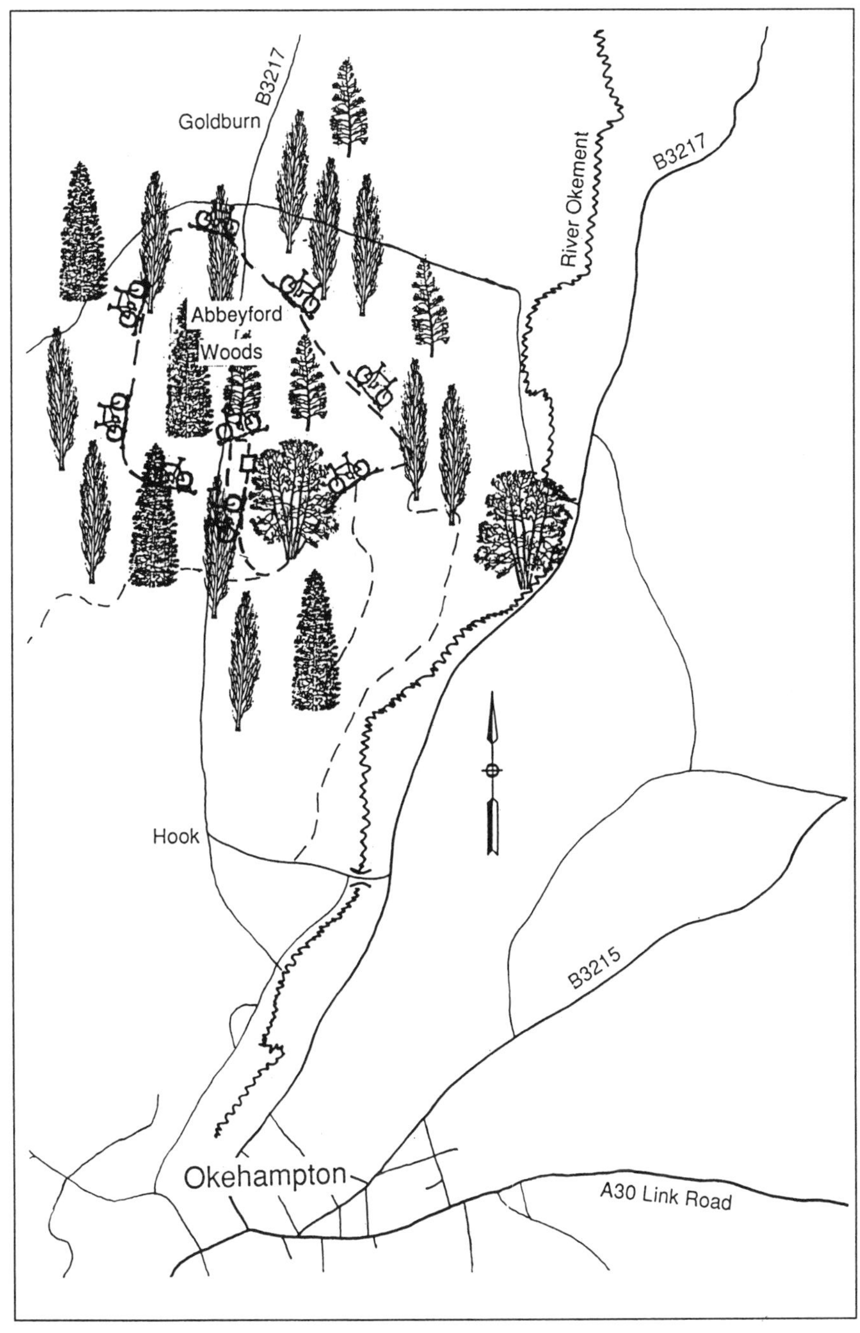
B3217
Goldburn
B3217
River Okement
Abbeyford
Woods
Hook
B3215
Okehampton
A30 Link Road

Access Points

Abbeyford Wood can be approached from either Okehampton in the South or from the A3072 in the North. There is car parking in the heart of the wood. The forest enjoys manageable gradients.

From Okehampton take the B3217 heading north from the main street and turn left onto the minor public road signposted Abbeyford Woods. After a short distance you will see the forestry car park on your right.

From the North and the A3072, take the minor road heading south from the village of Jacobstowe. Follow this for two or three miles until you see the car park on your left.

The Route

The WHITE waymarked route sets out from south east corner of the car park. This will lead to the road from where you must decide if you are in a clockwise mood or an anti-clockwise mood. There are interpretative information boards in the car park.

For the less energetic or non-cyclists in your party, a short walk south from the car park will lead to the broadleaf woodland where you will see a lovely collection of interesting mature tree species and, if you are still and patient, some wildlife.

If you want a change from pure forest riding, one of the most pleasant rides in the vicinity is not in the forest itself, but up and down the beautiful Borthwick Water Valley Approach Road as it leads away from the forest and back towards the B711. This is not a through route for vehicles, so enjoys very light traffic flow.

Nearby

The Tarka Trail skirts the eastern fringe of Abbeyford Wood. This is a 180-mile long-distance footpath leading from the high moors of Dartmoor to the north coast beyond Exmoor. The name is taken from the otter character of Henry Williamson's novels whose adventures were set in the Taw and Torridge valleys.

Ride 17

The Military Range Road, Okehampton Camp, Dartmoor, Devon.

A circuit around the tarmac military range road across an unspoilt and beautifully wild part of Dartmoor.

Maps: Landranger 1:50,000 series. Sheet numbers 00 and 11.

Distance: Total return ride 11 miles (18 km).

Waymarked: No, the ride follows a clearly defined roadway.

Gradients: A steep climb out of Okehampton which can be avoided if you start by driving up onto the moor and parking near the entrance to Okehampton Camp, but you will miss a super ride down at the end of the ride. The rest of the ride is undulating.

General surface description: Tarmac with some stone sections.

Future proposals:.N/A

Other cycle routes linking: N/A

Bicycle hire: Okehampton.

Shops and refreshments: Okehampton.

Special comments: There are far more non-firing days than firing days. There are many unlisted non-firing days.

Special warnings: Heed warning posts and signals. Danger areas are marked on the open ground by a series of red and white posts and on the main approaches by 'warning' notices. These indicate the limit of safe approach to the range danger areas. When firing is in progress you will see warning signals by way of red flags by day and red lights by night.

Permits: The ministry of defence welcomes public access to its land at all times except when live firing is taking place.

Needless to say, entry in a live firing area is forbidden and highly dangerous. When no warning signals are displayed, it is quite safe to enter the danger areas. Specific NON FIRING days are listed as follows: every Saturday, Sunday and Monday plus public holidays, all of April, May, July and August, the first fifteen days of September and the 20th December to 3rd of January inclusive. The warning notices also ask visitors not to pick up any metal objects within the firing range and there have been cases of children picking up World War II mortars 50 years after they were used. Buried live rounds can take that long to work their way to the surface.

The military training areas on Dartmoor account for 12,950 hectares (32,000 acres) of largely unspoilt wild moorland, about one third of the total moor. The northern part of Dartmoor around Okehampton Camp has been used for military training for the best part of two centuries, the earliest recorded use being in the early 19th century during the Napoleonic wars. A permanent camp was built in the early 1890s just south of Okehampton while the War Office, as it was then, used a large tract of land to the north of Okehampton for artillery firing. In one form or another, the military have stayed here ever since.

The ride utilises a tarmac military road which runs in a loop on the top of the this beautifully unspoilt part of Dartmoor. It dips up and down undulating between rocky stream-beds and at its high points it offers the rider some of the most magnificent views in Devon. The moor can be a very desolate and exposed place in

On the moors above Okehampton Camp

inclement weather so it would be best to wait for a dry day with light winds before tackling the route.

Most of the ride is on a tarmac surface but there are some rough stony sections which may cause some difficulty to narrow-wheeled bicycles. Take a camera and take your time, as this is a very enjoyable and rewarding ride.

Access Points

There are good car parks in Okehampton and if you wish to avoid the steep one-mile climb out of the town, there are places to park on the roadside, on the moor.

The Route

1. Leave Okehampton on Station Road, signed to Okehampton Camp. There is a steady steep climb for the best part of a mile but it's worth the effort, because you'll come down at a tremendous speed when you return at the end of the ride and steep climbs are always best tackled with fresh legs. If you decide to take the easier option, it is possible to park a car at the top at this climb and ride from there.
2. After crossing the railway and the main A30 road, the road flattens out and you will see the military camp ahead.
3. Keep left at the fork, keeping the camp on your right.
4. At a 'T' junction, turn left and cross the cattle grid and carry straight on through the ford.
5. Continue straight ahead until the road forks. Go left or right as you please. you will eventually arrive back at this same spot, as long as you keep to the road, your route to Okehampton.

A note of reassurance: Army range clearers collect livestock (and cyclists!), erect warning notices and fly flags before live firing commences. Observers maintain a constant and vigilant watch while exercises are taking place.

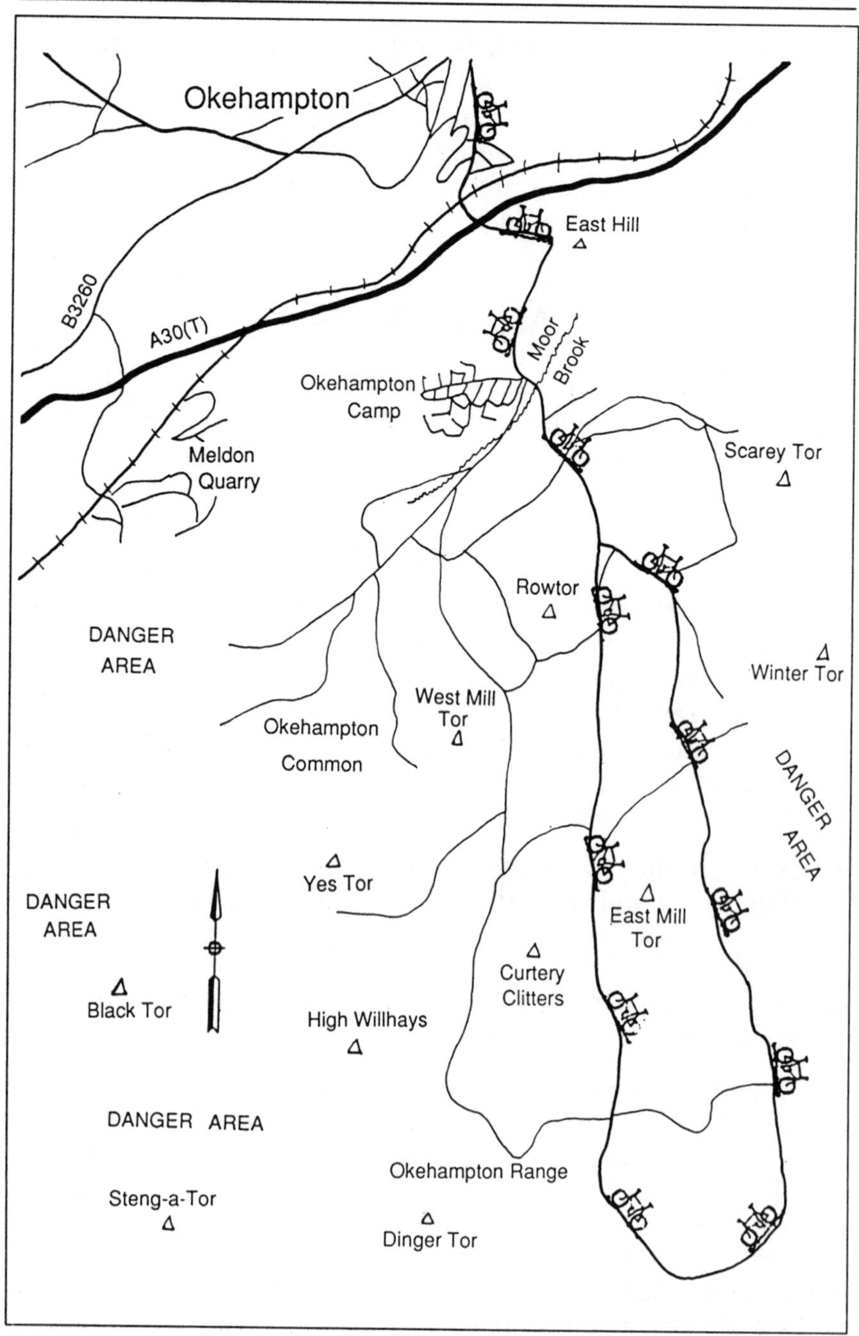
Okehampton
East Hill
B3260
A30(T)
Moor Brook
Okehampton Camp
Meldon Quarry
Scarey Tor
Rowtor
DANGER AREA
Winter Tor
West Mill Tor
Okehampton Common
DANGER AREA
Yes Tor
DANGER AREA
East Mill Tor
Curtery Clitters
Black Tor
High Willhays
DANGER AREA
Okehampton Range
Steng-a-Tor
Dinger Tor

Nearby

Over the years, military land holdings on the moor have tended to fluctuate according to the need of the times, the most intense use being during the 1939 to 1944 World War II period, when virtually all of Dartmoor was given over to military training. All three armed services use the moor as well as territorial and reserve forces and cadet organisations. The main landowner on the moor is the Duchy of Cornwall whose estate comprises a massive 28,330 hectares (70,000 acres) including most of the high moorland and central upland farms.

The whole moor is renowned for its wild scenic beauty as well as its ecological and archaeological importance. Some of highest land in England can be seen close to the route. As you cross a cattle grid to enter the military range, the high ground on your right is Yes Tor at 619 metres (2028 feet) above sea level. Just out of sight behind Yes Tor is High Willhays which at 621 metres (2039 feet) is the highest point in England south of Kinder Scout in the Peak District, which rises to 636 meters (2086 feet) nearly 250 miles to the north.

Ride 18

The Sticklepath Cycle Route, West Devon.

A waymarked cycle route around the peaceful lush Devon lanes and sleepy villages North of Dartmoor.

Maps: Landranger 1:50,000 series. Sheet numbers 191.

Distance: Total return ride 34 miles (54 km).

Waymarked: Signposts and finger posts 'Sticklepath Cycle Route'.

Gradients: There are a few climbs and descents along the route but also a lot of level riding.

General surface description: Tarmac.

Future proposals: N/A

Other cycle routes linking: Ride 16 (Abbeyford Woods).

Bicycle hire: Okehampton.

Shops and refreshments: Plenty of opportunities along the route. If you are planning to take a full day on the ride, which is recommended, a convenient lunch stop is Hatherleigh. Here you will find all of the essential requisites of a semi-tired cyclist.

Special comments: N/A

Special warnings: Normal road and traffic rules. *Be seen* and assume the driver of that car is blind or drunk or both.

Permits: N/A

The West Devon Sticklepath Cycle Route takes its name from the lovely and fascinating village of Sticklepath. This is genuine Devon at its very best, narrow lanes with high banked earthwork hedges, wild flowers, sleepy villages, a backdrop of Dartmoor and if you chose the right day, sunshine and bird-song to help you on your way. The route is based on the two river valleys of the Taw and the Okement and takes best advantage of the natural scenic beauty of the area.

The valleys offer shelter from the changeable conditions of nearby Dartmoor. If the weather is on the blustery side, this is normally a nice sheltered ride and if the weather is warm, there is plenty of shade cover. Do not rush the trip, stop occasionally to look at the beauty and listen to the peace; it is a rare commodity. This is a full day's ride and does involve a certain amount of climbing so be prepared for the occasional strenuous section.

It is interesting to observe the slow change of character of the rural scene as you venture further away from Dartmoor. Belstone and South Zeal, for instance, are predominately granite villages whilst in Sampford Courtenay, the cottages are cob and thatch. The landscape softens as you move north and the vegetation becomes more luxurious. This ride and its signposting is laid out by the local tourism authority with the aim of encouraging cycling in the area and is described in the leaflet 'West Devon Sticklepath Cycle Route'. It is well thought out, if a little long for some cyclists and possibly a little hilly for others. It gives an excellent insight into the area.

Signposts on the Sticlepath

Access Points

The starting point of the ride as described here is from Okehampton. Another good starting point would be the Tarka Centre at the Museum of Water-Power in Sticklepath but you could start from any one of the villages mentioned along the route. The directions are anti-clockwise to avoid as many right-hand turns as possible.

The Route

This route is very well waymarked.

1. From the main shopping street in Okehampton, head east and turn sharp left, signed for North Road Industrial Estate and Exbourne. This will take you along Northfield Road passing terraced houses.
2. At the 'T' junction, turn right, signed for Exbourne and North Road Industrial Estate. Leave the town through the small industrial area and past a short line of bungalows.
3. Pass through the village of Brightley and just after the thatched cottage and the Exbourne junction on the left, take the unsignposted narrow lane climbing up to the right.
4. At the crossroads go straight ahead down another unsignposted narrow lane.
5. At the 'T' junction, turn right.
6. Continue straight ahead at the next junction, signed for Belstone.
7. Turn right at the junction towards Belstone and Sticklepath.
8. Just after crossing over the A30, go straight on at the crossroads signed for Belstone.
9. Pass over the cattle grid onto Dartmoor National Park and in Belstone Village, go left (signed Skaigh and Sticklepath) and follow the road marked 'unsuitable for heavy goods vehicles'.
10. Cross the cattle grid into Sticklepath and turn right along the main road to Whiddon Down and Exeter.
11. Fork left in the village past Finch Foundry, by Tawside House Bed and Breakfast, towards South Zeal.
12. In South Zeal, turn left opposite the old chapel and head for South Tawton.
13. Go left at the 'T' junction and almost immediately right following the signs to South Tawton.
14. Go through the village leaving the Parish Church to your left

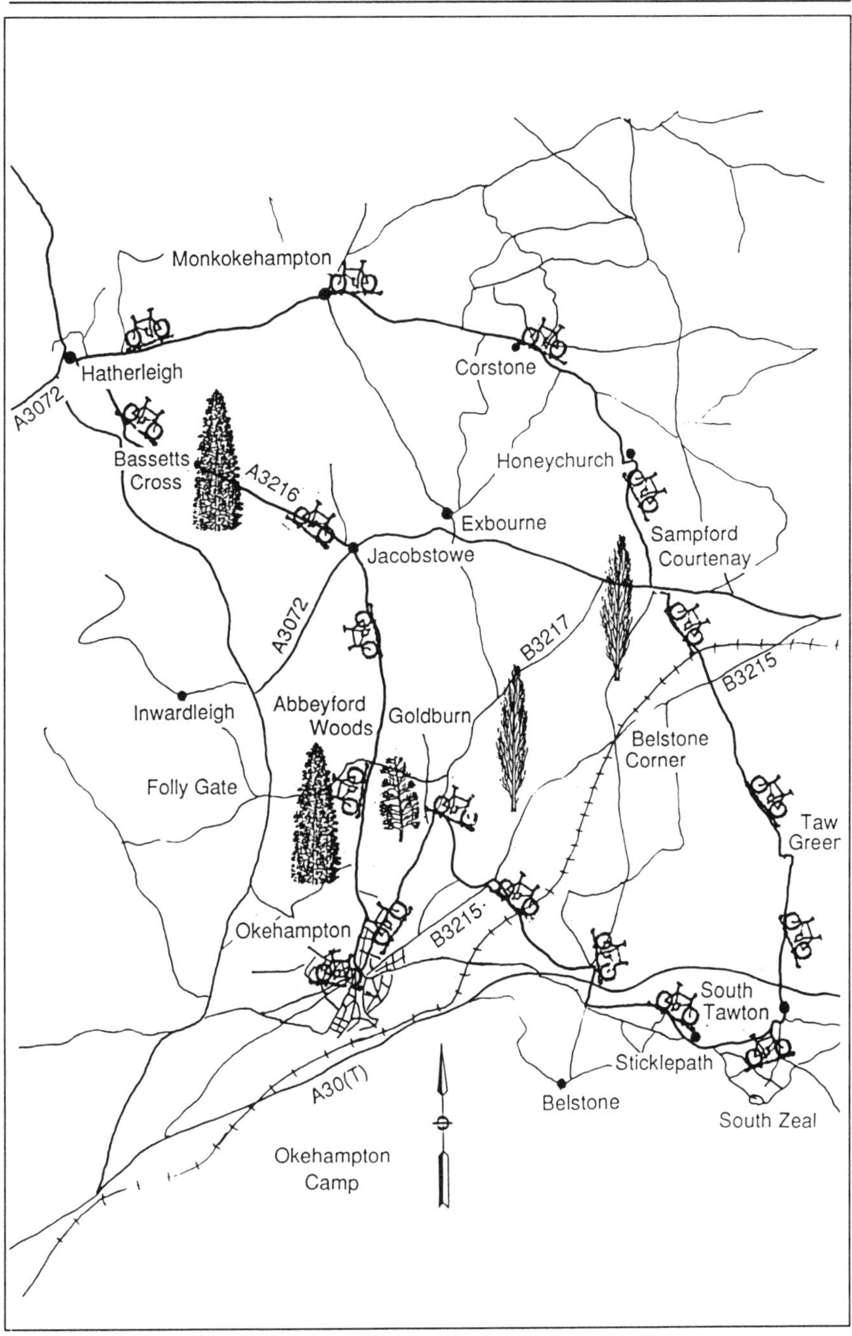

Monkokehampton
Hatherleigh
A3072
Corstone
Bassetts Cross
A3216
Honeychurch
Exbourne
Jacobstowe
Sampford Courtenay
A3072
B3217
B3215
Inwardleigh
Abbeyford Woods
Goldburn
Belstone Corner
Folly Gate
Taw Greer
Okehampton
B3215
South Tawton
Sticklepath
A30(T)
Belstone
South Zeal
Okehampton Camp

and following the signs for Wood and Spreyton. Once again cross the A30.

15. Continue, following the signs to Wood and Taw Green.
16. Turn left by Taw Green Baptist Chapel towards Halford and Langabeer. Follow this lane over the old stone bridge.
17. Turn right at the next 'T' junction towards Halford and Rowden.
18. Go straight on at Beacon Cross crossroads signed Fullaford and Trecott down the narrow weight-limited lane.
19. Follow through Trecott to the A3072 and turn left to Sampford Courtenay.
20. Go right in the village by the pub and pass through the village, leaving the church on the right.
21. Carry straight on at the next junction and left at the next junction following the signs for Honeychurch.
21. Go past the church on the right and at the 'T' junction go left towards Corstone Follow this road following signs to Monkokehampton.
22. In the village of Monkokehampton go left at the 'T' junction and then immediately right signed Hatherleigh.
23. Follow this road out of the village and follow the road to Hatherleigh.
24. In Hatherleigh go left along Higher Street and follow this road out of the village.
25. At the 'T' junction with the B3216, go left along the B3216 towards Crediton and North Tawton and follow this road to Jacobstowe.
26. In Jacobstowe turn right very briefly along the A3072 and then immediately left down the unsigned road towards Abbeyford Woods.
27. After passing through Abbeyford Woods, go right at the 'T' junction towards Okehampton and follow this road back to the town centre.

Nearby

History students will recognise the name ‘Sampford Courtenay’. This village is famed for the 1594 uprising against the introduction of an English translation of the traditional Latin prayer book – ‘The Prayer Book Rebellion’ – if only life were so simple today.

Sticklepath village is famed for its association with water power and it is well worth visiting the four water wheels that are still operating there today. The local industry of this area directly north of the moor was copper mining. As you ride through Sticklepath, try to call into the Museum of Water Power.

Ride 19

Chagford to the High Moor, Dartmoor, Devon.

Around a reservoir, through a forest and onto the high moor from the delightful ancient Stannary town of Chagford.

Maps: Landranger 1:50,000 series. Sheet number 191.

Distance: Total return ride 16 miles (26 km).

Waymarked: The route is on very quiet public roads and bridleways.

Gradients: A gentle climb to the high moorland. A refreshing descent all the way back. Take your time going up and look forward to to ride back down.

General surface description: Tarmac and forestry road.

Future proposals: N/A

Other cycle routes linking: There are plenty of optional routes in the forest. If you have some time you could easily spend an afternoon here. There are also bridleways across the high moor but watch the weather and beware of the military live firing ranges west and north west of the forest.

Bicycle hire: Okehampton.

Shops and refreshments: There are some fine tea shops and pubs in Chagford as well as a charming collection of shops.

Special comments: N/A

Special warnings: Be especially careful on the high moorland and in fog or inclement weather, take care to stay on the comparative safety of the bridleway.

Permits: N/A

Chagford is one of Devon's most ancient towns and until 1897 was a Stannary town. The word 'stannary' derives from the Latin 'stannum' meaning 'tin'. Chagford was the capital of one of the four local Stannaries, the tin-mining districts of Devon and Cornwall, the other capitals being Tavistock, Ashburton and Plympton. The Stannaries had their own courts with jurisdiction of the local law and taxation although very serious cases, such as murder, were normally referred to higher courts.

The ride leads away from Chagford to the west and over some

pleasant low moorland before ringing Fernworthy reservoir and climbing through the forest onto the high moor. The moor in this area is scattered with prehistoric stone circles and one of the best examples can be seen on the high moor at Scorhill.

There are some marvellous old buildings in Chagford including many excellent examples of genuine Tudor and Georgian architecture. One of the most impressive buildings is the Three Crowns Hotel with its massive thatched roof.

Access Points

There is a very good car park in Chagford and the route description is given from there. In the summer, Chagford can become very clogged up with tourists' cars so it may well be worth considering basing your ride from the car park at Fernworthy reservoir. If you do this, head for Chagford first and tackle the forest section last. This will ensure a downhill finish for your tired legs.

Through the forest to High Dartmoor

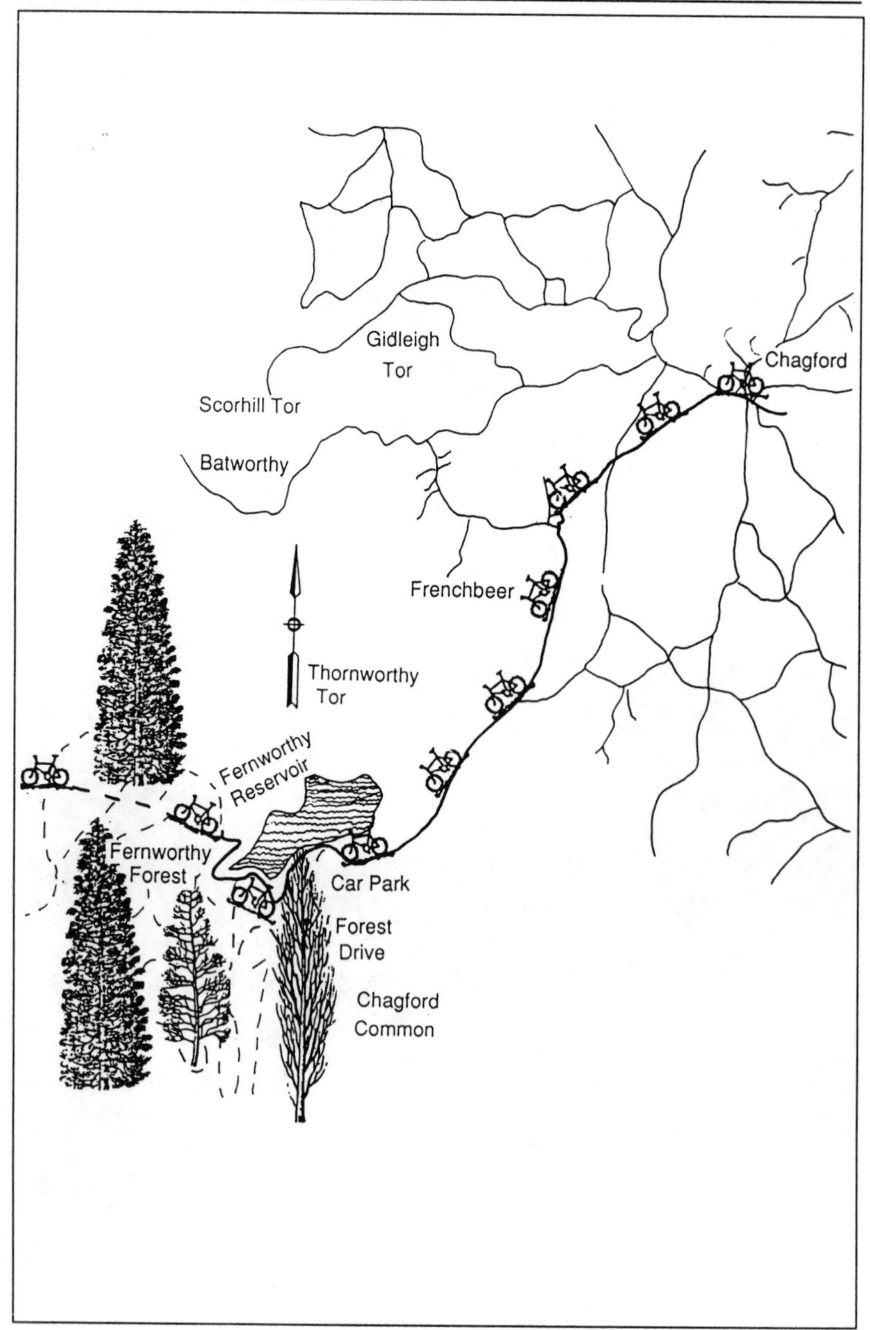
Gidleigh
Tor
Scorhill Tor
Batworthy
Chagford
Frenchbeer
Thornworthy
Tor
Fernworthy
Reservoir
Fernworthy
Forest
Car Park
Forest
Drive
Chagford
Common

The Route

1. Turn left out of Chagford car park, passing the church to your right.
2. Go right at the 'T' junction and continue through the village past the interesting selection of old shops.
3. Follow the sign posts to Fernworthy Reservoir.
4. After about one and half miles, take the right-hand fork. Proceed across the cattle grid onto the low moor.
5. Keep straight ahead past Fernworthy Reservoir and follow the road around its far perimeter.
6. Where the tarmac road ends, turn left into the forest along the bridle way marked 'To the Moor'.
7. Turn left at the 'T' in the bridleway and follow the track until you reach the high moor.
8. Turn and retrace your track to Chagford, mostly a gentle descent.

Nearby

Northwest of Chagford is the lovely village of Gidleigh which boasts the remains of a small castle. To the east of Chagford is the delightful market town of Moretonhampstead and to the northwest of here is Cranbrook Castle, an Iron Age hill fort 1100 feet over the River Teign.

Ride 20

Bere Peninsula Cycle Route, West Devon.

A nine-mile circular cycle ride around the forgotten and very peaceful silver-mining areas of the Bere Peninsula.

Maps: Landranger 1:50,000 series. Sheet number 201.

Distance: Total return ride 9 miles (14.5 km).

Waymarked: 'Bere Peninsula Cycle Route' with signs and finger posts.

Gradients: A few steep, sharp short gradients as the route climbs and descends the sides of the river valleys but generally a pleasant and easy ride.

General surface description: Tarmac.

Future proposals: N/A

Other cycle routes linking: N/A

Bicycle hire: Tavistock, Plymouth.

Shops and refreshments: Main facilities in Bere Alston and in Bere Ferrers.

Special comments: N/A

Special warnings: Although the traffic conditions are generally very light, do not forget that you are on a public road and *be seen!*

Permits: N/A

The Bere Peninsula is one of the least visited parts of West Devon. This is mainly because of its geographical location, isolated from Plymouth to the south, Cornwall to the west and Tavistock to the east by tidal stretches of the rivers Tamar and Tavy. From Plymouth railway station, a train journey to Bere Ferrers takes only 17 minutes and includes 4 other stops over the 7 mile distance, this by virtue of the Tavy railway bridge. With no road bridges or ferries, the same trip by car will take over 45 minutes and involve a drive of nearly 22 miles. This lack of easy accessibility has created an unusually beautiful and largely unspoilt, peaceful backwater flanked by long frontages onto magnificent stretches of the Tamar and Tavy rivers.

Although it may seem difficult to believe today, the area was once a busy industrial mining centre with great reserves of lead and silver in the mines which extended under the River Tamar. The earliest references to these mining activities date back to the 13th century. The mines came to sudden halt one Sunday in 1856 when the Tamar burst into the underground workings. Because of the general decline of reserves, it was not considered economical to sink new shafts.

This is a moderately easy half-day ride and although it is entirely on public roads, the traffic is extremely light and therefore unlikely to spoil your cycling. Take your time and enjoy the surroundings, particularly on the tidal riverside sections where you will have a chance to see some wonderful bird-life, particularly herons. Industrial archaeologists will enjoy seeing the remains of a once-vibrant silver and lead mining industry and the effect of the London and South Western Railway on the landscape of the peninsula. This ride and its signposting is laid out by the local tourism authority with the aim of encouraging cycling in the area and is described in the leaflet 'West Devon Bere Peninsula Cycle Route'. It is well conceived and gives an excellent insight into this lovely peninsula.

Good signs on the Bere Peninsula

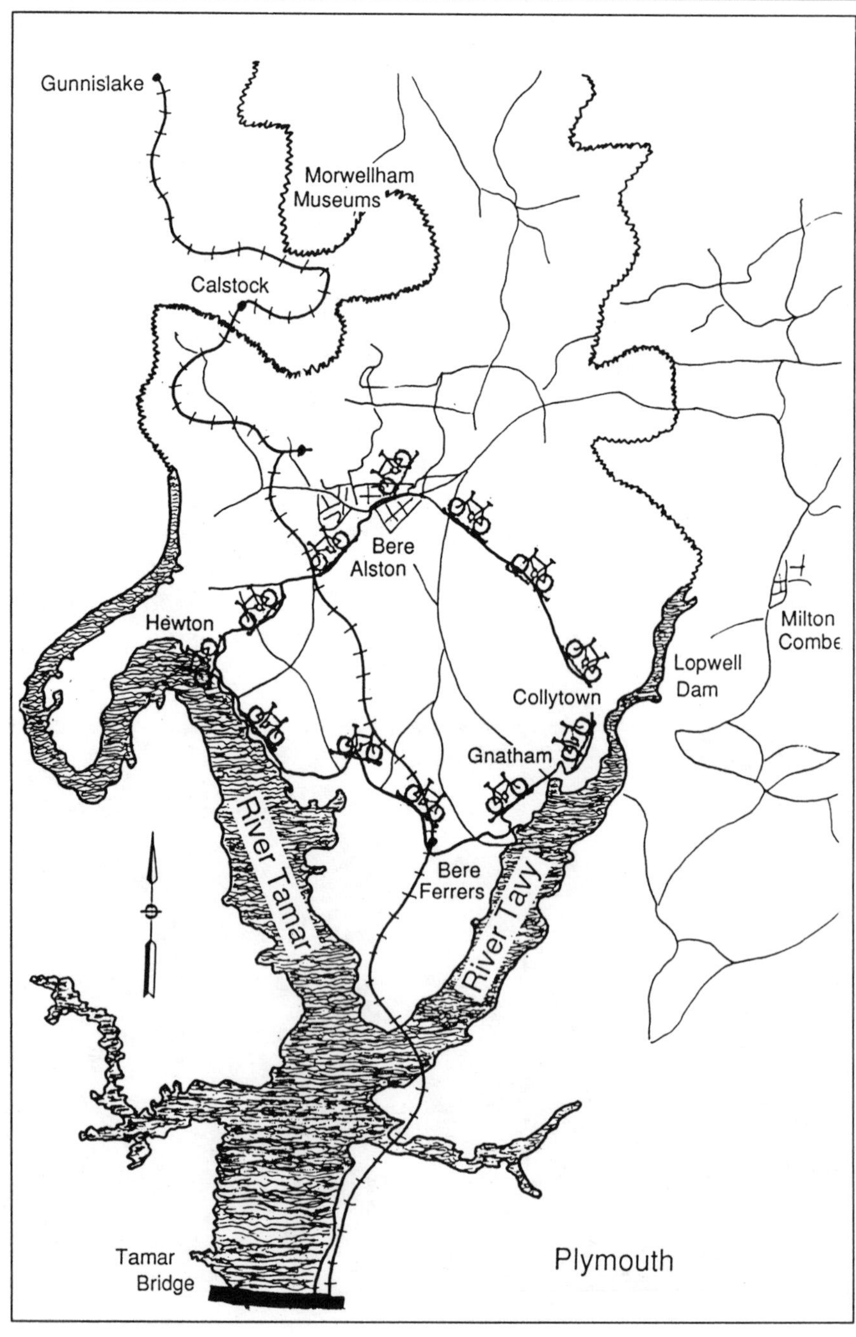
Gunnislake
Morwellham
Museums
Calstock
Bere
Alston
Hewton
Collytown
Gnatham
Lopwell
Dam
Milton
Combe
River Tamar
Bere
Ferrers
River Tavy
Tamar
Bridge
Plymouth

Access Points

The starting point of the ride is from Pilgrim Drive car park in Bere Alston. You could equally well start from anywhere along the route; Bere Ferrers would be a good alternative. The directions are anti-clockwise to avoid as many right-hand turns as possible.

The Route

(The whole route is clearly waymarked with signs and finger posts.)

1. Starting from Pilgrim Drive car park in Bere Alston, follow Pilgrim Drive back to the junction with Bedford Street and turn left.
2. Turn left through the village following the road around to left via Fore Street and passing the church on your left.
3. Turn right into Pentillie Road and follow the road over the rail bridge to Hole's Hole and Hewton.
4. After the descent to the banks of the Tamar at Hole's Hole, follow the road alongside the river until it turns inland at Clamoak.
5. Follow the road to Bere Ferrers.
6. In the village, turn right (opposite Bere Ferrers Social Club) to the banks of the River Tavy.
7. Follow the road to Gnatham and then uphill to Collytown. From here is an easy ride to return to Bere Alston.

Nearby

Hole's Hole was once a stop for the paddle steamer that served Devonport and Plymouth. Baskets were made here to carry the produce from the market gardens of the peninsula. Just south of Hole's Hole is Weir Quay which served the mining activities of the area.

A monument at Bere Ferrers station is to the memory of eighteen New Zealand soldiers who were killed in an awful railway disaster here in 1915.

Ride 21

The West Devon (Tavistock) Cycle Route

A choice of 26 or 11 mile routes based from Tavistock on the western fringes of Dartmoor.

Maps: Landranger 1:50,000 series. Sheet number 201.

Distance: Total return rides 26 or 11 miles (42 or 18 km).

Waymarked: 'West Devon Cycle Route' with signs and finger posts.

Gradients: The ride climbs fairly continuously to Lydford. After undulating for a while with the occasional short steep gradient, the ride generally slopes down to return to Tavistock. In summary, a few steep gradients and a few long and gradual gradients.

General surface description: Tarmac.

Future proposals: N/A

Other cycle routes linking: N/A

Bicycle hire: Tavistock.

Shops and refreshments: Plenty of chances as you pass through villages along the route.

Special comments: N/A

Special warnings: This is an on-road route. *Be seen.*

Permits: N/A

This is a moderate half- or full-day ride, depending on which distance is chosen. It is entirely on public roads, but the traffic is fairly light and unlikely to spoil your cycling. Take your time and enjoy the surroundings, particularly Lydford Gorge, Quither Common and the volcanic Brent Tor. A visit to the 12th-century church of St Michael de Rupe on top of the tor is highly recommended; the views on a clear day are fantastic. There are many sections along the ride where you may see some wonderful wild flowers.

This is a ride which can easily be divided into two or three sections to suit your time schedule and energy reserves. If you only want a short ride, take the diversion at Brent Tor and enjoy Quither Common and the descent into Tavistock. The surroundings are truly magnificent and because of the magnet of Dartmoor to the east, the area is not crowded either in terms of people or traffic. There can surely be few better areas to be riding a bicycle.

There is a good variation of riding, a fascinating amount of interest and, in the right weather conditions, unbelievable views in many directions. On a clear day you will see the steep flanks of Dartmoor and the granite tors which are so distinctive to the area. You will pass through wooded valleys and along quiet lanes linking sleepy villages and isolated farms. This ride and its signposting is laid out by the local tourism authority with the aim of encouraging cycling in the area and is described in the leaflet 'West Devon (Tavistock) Cycle Route'. It is well thought out, if a little hilly in places, and gives an excellent feel for the area.

Access Points

The starting point of the ride is from the Tourist Information Centre in Bedford Square, Tavistock. You can start from any point along the route. Lydford would be a good alternative but most cyclists will prefer the prospect of starting their day's riding at the bottom of a climb. The directions are anti-clockwise to avoid as many right-hand turns as possible.

The Tavistock Cycle Route

The Route

(The route is well waymarked with signs and finger posts.)

1. Starting from the tourist information centre in Bedford Square, Tavistock, follow the signed to Brentor Chillaton Lewdown and Lifton and leave Tavistock on the road that climbs away between two banks via Butcher Park Road.
2. Proceed out of town under the impressive stone viaduct.
3. At Brent Tor continue straight ahead – or for the short 11 mile route go left here (signed Milton Abbot and Brentor Church) to then rejoin the main route by turning left at the next crossroads at Quither.
4. Assuming you are completing the full route, follow the signs to Lydford and proceed past Lydford Gorge and into Lydford village, proceeding through the village and past Lydford Castle.
5. Turn left at the war memorial.
6. Bear left at the fork a few yards further on signed to Coryton.
7. Follow the signs for Coryton and continue past Lydford Woods following signs for Lowertown and Coryton Church.
8. Continue straight on at the crossroads signed for Sydenham and Port Gate.
9. After passing the edge of Sydenham Wood, turn left, towards Sydenham and Marystow and proceed over the old bridge.
10. At Stewardry Cross, continue straight ahead for Chillaton.
11. At the 'T' junction turn right to Chillaton and continue over the narrow stone bridge.
12. At the next 'T' junction, go left (signed Chillaton and Tavistock) and continue into the village of Chillaton.
13. In the centre of the village, at the junction by the Chichester Arms Public House, go straight on at the cross roads, taking the little road to the left of the Public House. Follow this lane around to the right after twenty yards and continue as it takes you behind the village.
14. At the 'T' junction, turn left onto the busier road.

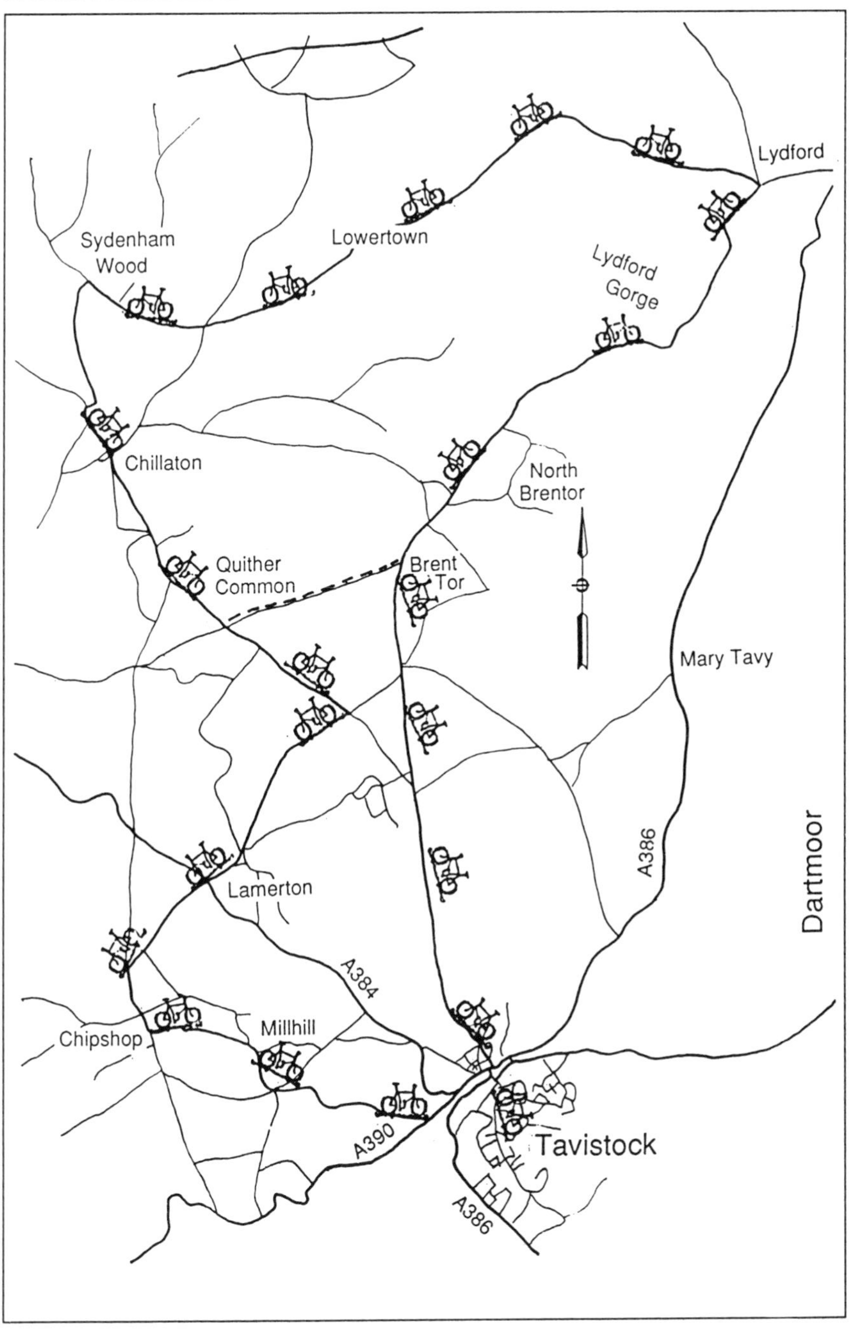
Lydford
Sydenham Wood
Lowertown
Lydford Gorge
Chillaton
North Brentor
Quither Common
Brent Tor
Mary Tavy
A386
Dartmoor
Lamerton
A384
Chipshop
Millhill
Tavistock
A390
A386

15. Continue towards Quither Common following the signs to Tavistock.
16. Pass the first crossroads on the left where the short-cut route joins from the left.
17. Turn right towards Lamerton.
18. Turn right at the crossroads signed Chipshop and Launceston.
19. In the village of Lamerton, go straight on at the crossroads of the B3362 down the unsignposted narrow lane.
20. At the 'T' junction, go left.
21. Go straight on at the crossroads in the hamlet of Chipshop and take the first left turn just beyond, down the unsignposted narrow lane.
22. At the 'T' junction turn right and then take the first right-hand turn just past Chapel Cottage.
23. At the crossroads, turn left towards Tavistock.
24. Keep right at the next fork. This road emerges into Tavistock as 'Crease Lane'. Where it joins the main road, keep left and follow the signs to the Town Centre.
25. This will return you to Bedford Square via Plymouth Road.

Nearby

Try to pay a visit to the Dartmoor and West Devon Information Centre in Tavistock. Here you will find a great deal of information and some fascinating facts about the area.

Lydford Gorge is one of the most stunning deep wooded gorges in Britain. For a small consideration to the National Trust, you will be allowed to use the steep paths to descend the Gorge to see either White Ladies Waterfall or The Devil's Cauldron (or both) On a quiet day when there are few visitors, the Gorge can be a magical place.

Tavistock Canal has undergone extensive renovation over recent years and a delightful way to explore it from the town centre is by hiring a little canoe for a couple of hours.

Ride 22

The Barbican Plymouth to the Edge of Dartmoor via the Plym Valley Cycleway.

A magnificent cycle way and valley railway path leading from the historic city of Plymouth to the beauty of lower Dartmoor.

Maps: Landranger 1:50,000 series. Sheet number 201.

Distance: Total return ride 22 miles (35½ km).

Waymarked: Yes, quite clearly with routed posts.

Gradients: There is a fairly easy constant climb to Dartmoor. It is nothing to worry about going up but is a delight coming back down. If you feel like a really easy bike ride, the one way trip, downwards from Clearwater to Saltram House must rank as a favourite choice. You will hardly need to pedal.

General surface description: Well-drained crushed stone or gravel.

Future proposals: Proposed extension in the South to Radford Lake.

Other cycle routes linking: A convenient link onto the "West Devon Bere Peninsula Cycle Route". Access by crossing Lapwell Dam at Bickleigh but check the tides!

Bicycle hire: Plymouth.

Shops and refreshments: Anywhere south of Plym Bridge and beyond at Bickleigh and Clearbrook.

Special comments: N/A

Special warnings: There are plenty of wild ponies on Dartmoor. If you feed them they can sometimes bite.

Permits: N/A

The Plym Valley Cycleway runs from Plymouth in a northerly direction up the River Plym Valley. Most of it runs along the disused trackbed of the South Devon and Tavistock Railway Company, a section of the Great Western Railway that formed part of a northerly route, across the top of Dartmoor and on to Exeter. Separate branch lines ran off the northerly leg respectively to Wadebridge and Bude. Both of these branches are now abandoned to rail traffic. The railway opened in 1859, the original work overseen by Brunel. It did fairly

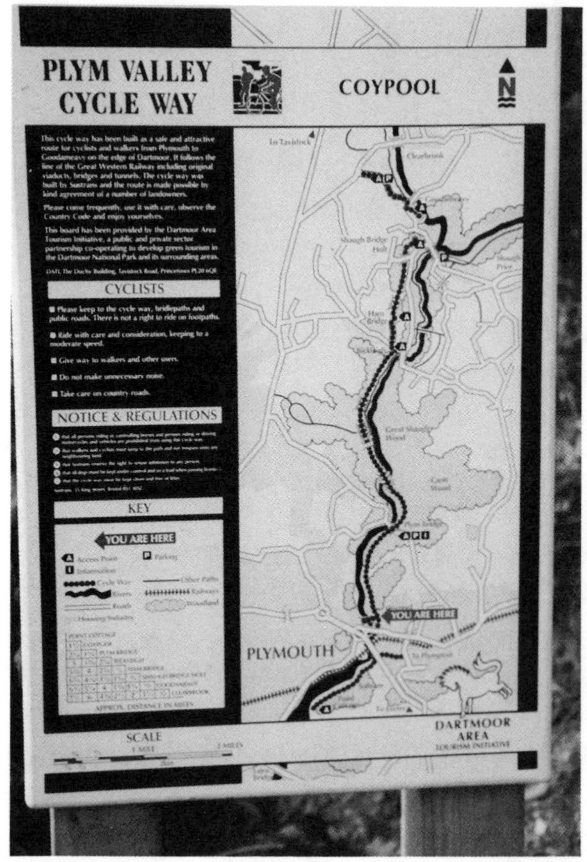

well serving the local mines and quarries but business declined to the point that the line closed down completely in 1956, a life of ninety-seven years.

The southern part of the trail into the Plymouth follows the eastern side of the Plym Estuary across the flat drained expanse of Chelston Meadow and on through the grounds of Saltram House which is in National Trust ownership and is one of Devon's largest country houses. The original house was built in the sixteenth century. The short section between Saltram House and the old GWR trackbed runs along the routes of the Lee Moor Tramway and then the Cann Tramway.

The route is virtually all off-road and has first-class, hard, well drained surfaces, conducive to enjoyable cycling. Features include a curved tunnel, for which you will require some form of lighting. Enjoy the thrill of crossing the original viaducts, one 97 feet high and another 123 feet high. Don't look down! There are also plenty of interesting cuttings and bridges. At the end of the route it's worth a little extra effort to climb the last half mile or so on to the barren edge of Dartmoor. Don't feed the wild ponies as they bite.

The trackbed was in a state of total disrepair when the initiative was taken to upgrade the route for use as a recreational footpath and cycleway. After a lot of negotiation with landowners a through route was established only relying on roads for a couple of unavoidable short stretches. The surface was compacted with crushed stone after substantial drainage and ancillary works were completed.

Access Points

The directions are given from the Barbican and as there is good car parking in this area of Plymouth and it is the lowest point of the ride, it is an ideal start and finish point. There are however many other good base points throughout the route. A very good alternative to the Barbican is the NT car park at Saltram House. From here go left of the house for Plymouth and the other way for the moor!

The Route

1. Leave the Barbican by passing over tide gate and follow the path straight ahead until it joins a residential road. The harbour is still close on the right.
2. Turn right into Cattledown Road and follow this around. The oil terminals will be below you on your right-hand side. The road eventually descends into an old industrial area.
3. Continue straight ahead to the 'T' junction and turn right.
4. Follow this road along the shared pedestrian/cycle lane. You will eventually come out at Laira Bridge.
5. Turn right over the bridge on the cycle lane provided and left at the eastern end.
6. Follow this road to the car park.
7. Turn left into the grounds of Saltram House. Follow the path with the river close on your left. From here you will pick up the signs to the Plym Valley Cycle Way.
8. After passing through the flat meadow land alongside the estuary of the River Plym you will eventually emerge to pass under the vast concrete flyover at Marsh Mills roundabout, which

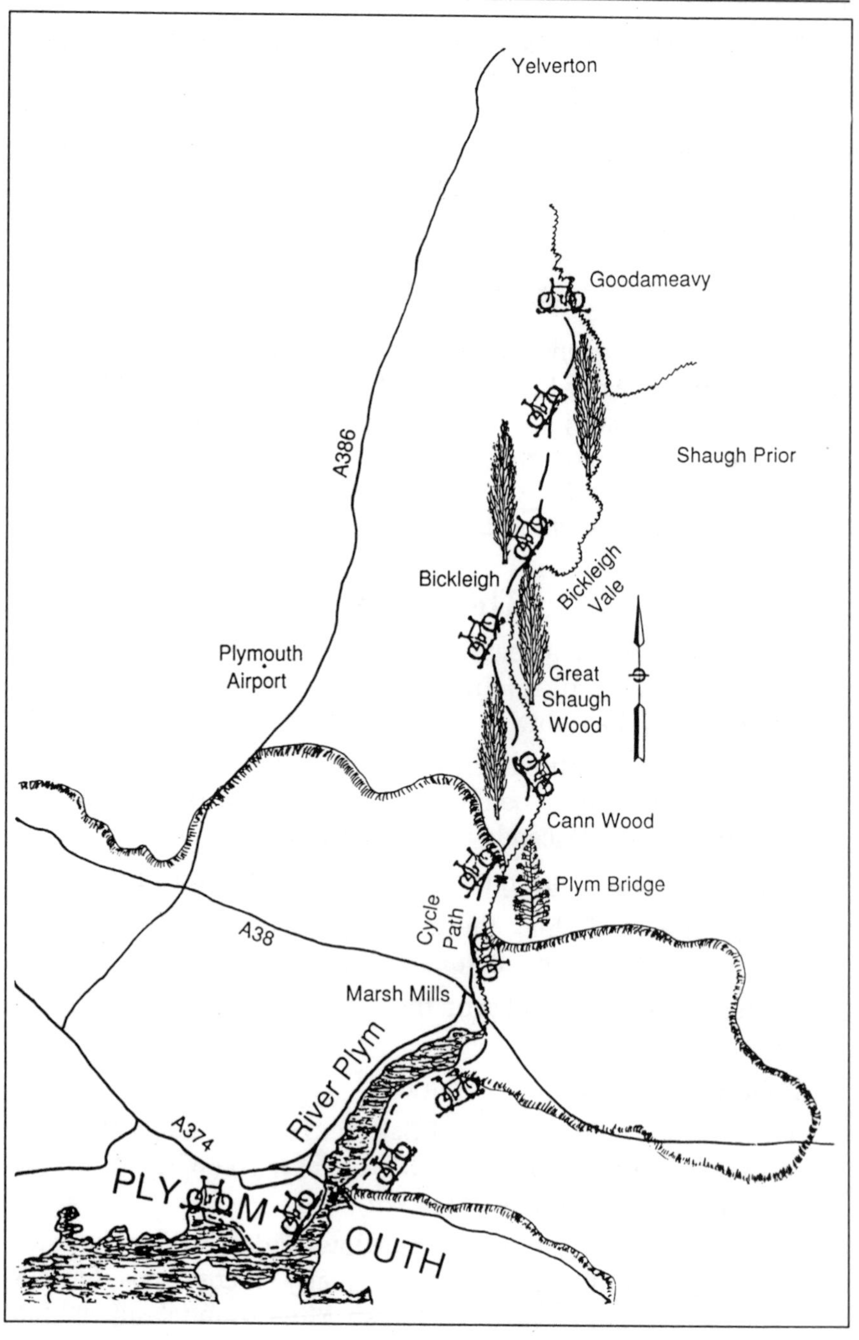
Yelverton
Goodameavy
Shaugh Prior
A386
Bickleigh
Bickleigh Vale
Plymouth Airport
Great Shaugh Wood
Cann Wood
Plym Bridge
Cycle Path
A38
Marsh Mills
River Plym
A374
PLYMOUTH

carries A38 traffic over our heads on its way towards the Tamar bridge and Cornwall in the west and Exeter in the east. Follow the signs towards the Royal Marines Barracks.

9. The first signs of the rail path are by the Royal Marines Barracks at Coypool. (Here enthusiasts are hoping to reopen a section of track to display some of their fine steam engines.) Try the café.
10. Follow the railway path, and as you proceed northwards through the woodland, you'll cross the Cann Viaduct and have a fine view into the valley below. It's easy here to imagine the hundreds of workers busily breaking slates and carting them away in the great Cann quarries. There's further woodland and two high viaducts before reaching a short on-road section at Bickleigh. A great view from here but just one of many en route.
11. After reverting to the road briefly at Bickleigh follow the signs to rejoin the railway path and enjoy another viaduct, not so high but the longest of the trail. Wind on through beautiful country and past more railway relics, including the clear remains of Shaugh Bridge Station.
12. Eventually you will arrive at the 308-yard-long Shaugh Tunnel. Unless you have eyes that can see in the dark, you will need a torch or bike light to avoid disaster.
13. Beyond the tunnel is the end of the railway path at Goodmeavy Bridge. Do take an hour or so to explore around the base of the moor.
14. Return as you came or follow the joint cycle/footpath past the strange-looking supermarket, to follow the west side of the Plym estuary from Marsh Mills roundabout back towards Laira Bridge in Plymouth.

Nearby

The two obvious attractions are at either end of the trail, Dartmoor at the top and Plymouth at the bottom. In each case, there is so much to see that you will need to make reference to local guide and tourist information.

Along the way notable points of interest are as follows: Chelston

Meadow, drained in 1806 to form a racecourse : Saltram House which used to belong to the infamously greedy Bagg Family and dates back to the sixteenth century : dense old woodland known as Henroost and Hatshill : Bickleigh Vale, a well known local beauty spot : the remains of Shaugh Bridge and Shaugh Iron Ore Mine as well as sidings at Shaugh Bridge : the remains of a nineteenth century iron aqueduct just south of Shaugh Tunnel.

Ride 23

Burrator Reservoir, Dartmoor, West Devon.

A delightful round reservoir and rural ride in the shadow of Dartmoor.

Maps: Landranger 1:50,000 series. Sheet number 201, 202.

Distance: Total return ride 10 miles (15½ km).

Waymarked: No.

Gradients: Mild.

General surface description: Tarmac.

Future proposals: N/A

Other cycle routes linking: N/A

Bicycle hire: Tavistock.

Shops and refreshments: Meavey, Yelverton, Sheepstor.

Special comments: N/A

Special warnings: N/A

Permits: N/A

This easy half-day ride is based on Yelverton, on the very edge of Dartmoor, and takes you through some typical English country lanes, through a couple of charming villages and around Burrator Reservoir, under the shadow of Sheepstor. Around the reservoir you will see mossy woodland and a hint of the wildness and close proximity of the moor from the presence of wild ponies grazing at the edge of the road, which is close to the water for most of the way. If the weather is hot, look forward to the head of the reservoir where you may rest by a shady rocky stream.

Because this is such a sheltered ride, it may be best kept in reserve for a day when Dartmoor has lost its charm. The pretty little village of Meavy is traditional England personified. Old mossy-roofed cottages overlook the village green and old stone cross. The old English church, the knurled tree and the pub set the perfect scene.

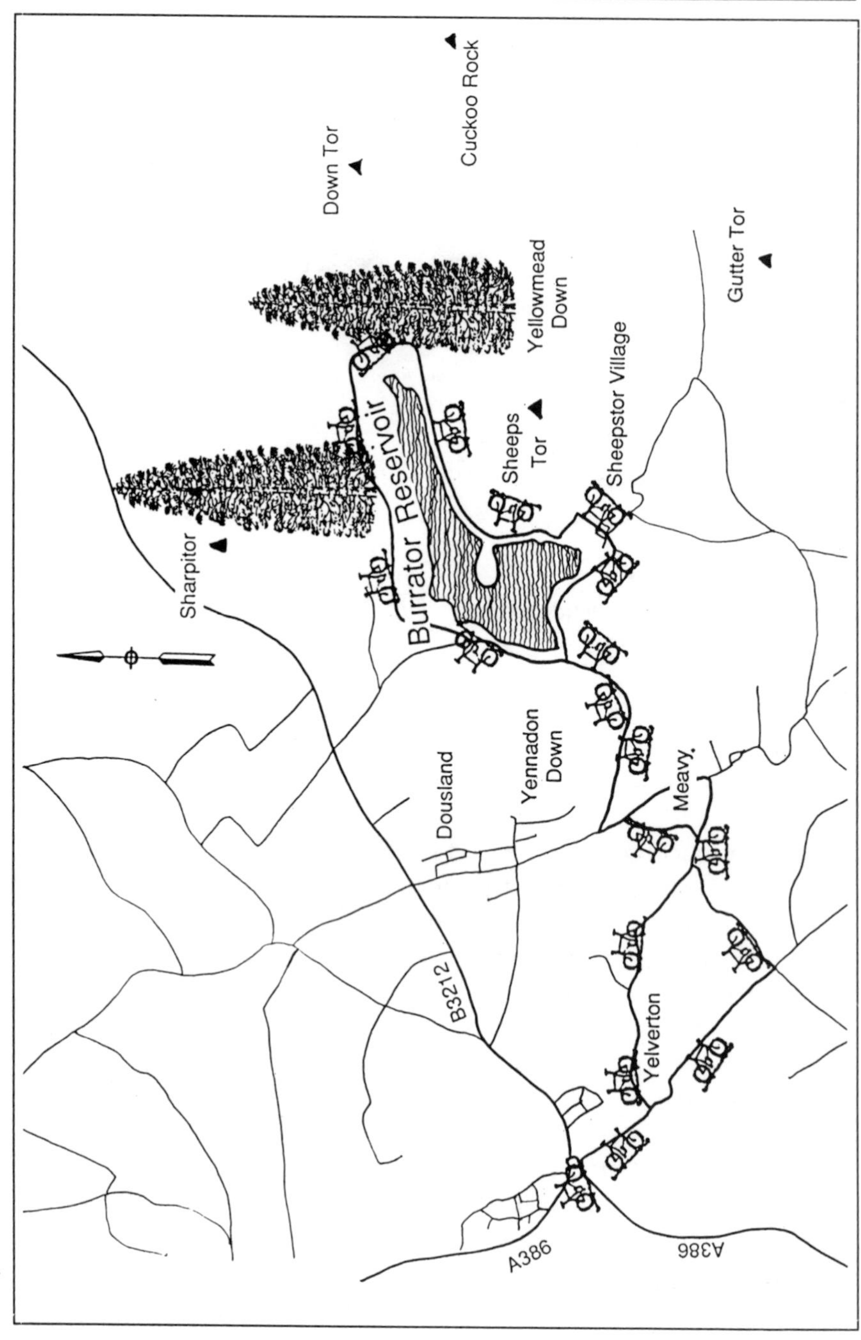
Cuckoo Rock
Down Tor
Yellowmead Down
Sheepstor Village
Gutter Tor
Sheeps Tor
Burrator Reservoir
Sharpitor
Dousland
Yennadon Down
Meavy
B3212
Yelverton
A386
A386

Three plaques, copied as they stand, set into the walls of the dam explain the history of the reservoir:

First Plaque "This plaque was, at the invitation of South West Water, unveiled by Neil McFarlan esq MP and parliamentary under secretary of state, department of the environment, on the 8th of June 1985 to mark the 400th anniversary of the act authorising construction of Drake's famous leat which was to convey water to Plymouth for over 300 years.".

Second Plaque (Borough of Plymouth, 1923-28). "This stone commemorates the enlargement of the reservoir from a capacity of 668 to 1026 million gallons."

Third Plaque. (Borough of Plymouth) "Burrator Reservoir commenced 1893 completed 1898."

Access Points

The starting point of this ride is from St Paul's Church in Yelverton. Alternatively, start from anywhere along the route; Meavey would be a good alternative for a shorter return ride. The directions are anti-clockwise to avoid as many right-hand turns as possible.

The Route

1. With your back to St Paul's Church in Yelverton, turn right towards the garage and shop.
2. Turn right down the lane before the garage, towards Cadover Bridge.
3. Carry straight on past the first left turn for Meavy and after two miles take the second turn signed Meavy.
4. Follow this lane downhill towards the village, you will see Meavy Church in the distance.
5. Shortly after crossing a bridge you will enter the village. Turn right and continue past the village green.
6. Turn left uphill (signed Douseland) and continue for for half a mile out of the village.

7. Take the right turn over the cattle grid towards Burrator Reservoir.
8. Pass over gentle boulder-strewn moorland before arriving at Burrator Dam.

Burrator Dam

9. Turn right over the dam and follow the road into the quiet village of Sheepstor.
10. Pass through the village.
11. After two-tenths of a mile take the unmarked turn to the left and after only a short distance you will find yourself following around the reservoir in an anti-clockwise direction.
12. From the dam, retrace your route to the cattle grid (straight on).
13. Turn left and then first right into Meavy.
14. Turn right through the village and carry straight on signed Yelverton.
15. After a mile and a half turn right to return to St Paul's Church.

Nearby

The old village of Meavy is particularly notable for the oak tree which stands in front of the church. It is reputed to have been planted when the church was new 900 years ago! On close inspection you will see that the tree is now no more than a shell. Locally it is said that nine men once dined inside the trunk. The church was rebuilt in the fifteenth century.

The great granite outcrop known as 'Sheeps Tor', which towers behind the village of Sheepstor, is one of the largest of the 170 tors of Dartmoor. Tors are geological features which can be described as granite towers formed in the earth's surface during rock formation. The granite being a harder material than the surrounding rock has weathered more slowly. The words 'tor' and 'tower' are both derived from the Celtic word for tower, 'twr'.

Ride 24

Bellever Forest, Dartmoor.

A short ride in one of Dartmoor's high forests amongst stone circles and by the rock-strewn East Dart River.

Maps: Landranger 1:50,000 series. Sheet number 191.

Distance: Total loop ride 3 miles (5 km).

Waymarked: Yes.

Gradients: Easy riding.

General surface description: Forestry tracks.

Future proposals: N/A

Other cycle routes linking: N/A

Bicycle hire: Tavistock.

Shops and refreshments: Postbridge.

Special comments: N/A

Special warnings: N/A

Permits: N/A

This short ride in one of Dartmoor's highest forests is ideal for helping with a fitness or training programme and is the perfect ride to introduce young cyclists to the joys of forest cycling. Situated just south of Postbridge village on the B3212. The forestry tracks are easily accessible from the Bellever car park facility which is approached from the village of Bellever village. The boulder-strewn bed of the East Dart River adds more charm to the forest and is a refreshing sight on a warm day.

Bellever forest is situated in the high central area of Dartmoor and was planted in 1921 by the Duchy of Cornwall. Ever present are the rugged Bellever and Laughter tors, which are granite outcrops eroded less by time than the surrounding softer rocks. Within the forest are the remains of several stone circles as well as remains of huts used by residents here over 2000 years ago.

Bellever Forest

The High Dartmoor Visitor centre in nearby Princetown is well worth a visit, offering general information as well as an excellent and highly informative presentation. This tells you all you are ever likely to want to know about the wildlife and trees in the Dartmoor forests as well as a great deal of fascinating information about Dartmoor in general.

Access Points

Bellever car park. Leave the B3212 west of Postbridge village, on the minor road to Bellever heading south. The forest is on your left-hand side. The car park is approached by turning right in Bellever village. There are information boards in the car park. There are also picnic facilities.

The Route

The waymarked route sets out from the south-east or north-west corners of the car park. You must decide if you are in a clockwise mood or an anti-clockwise mood. There are interpretative informa-

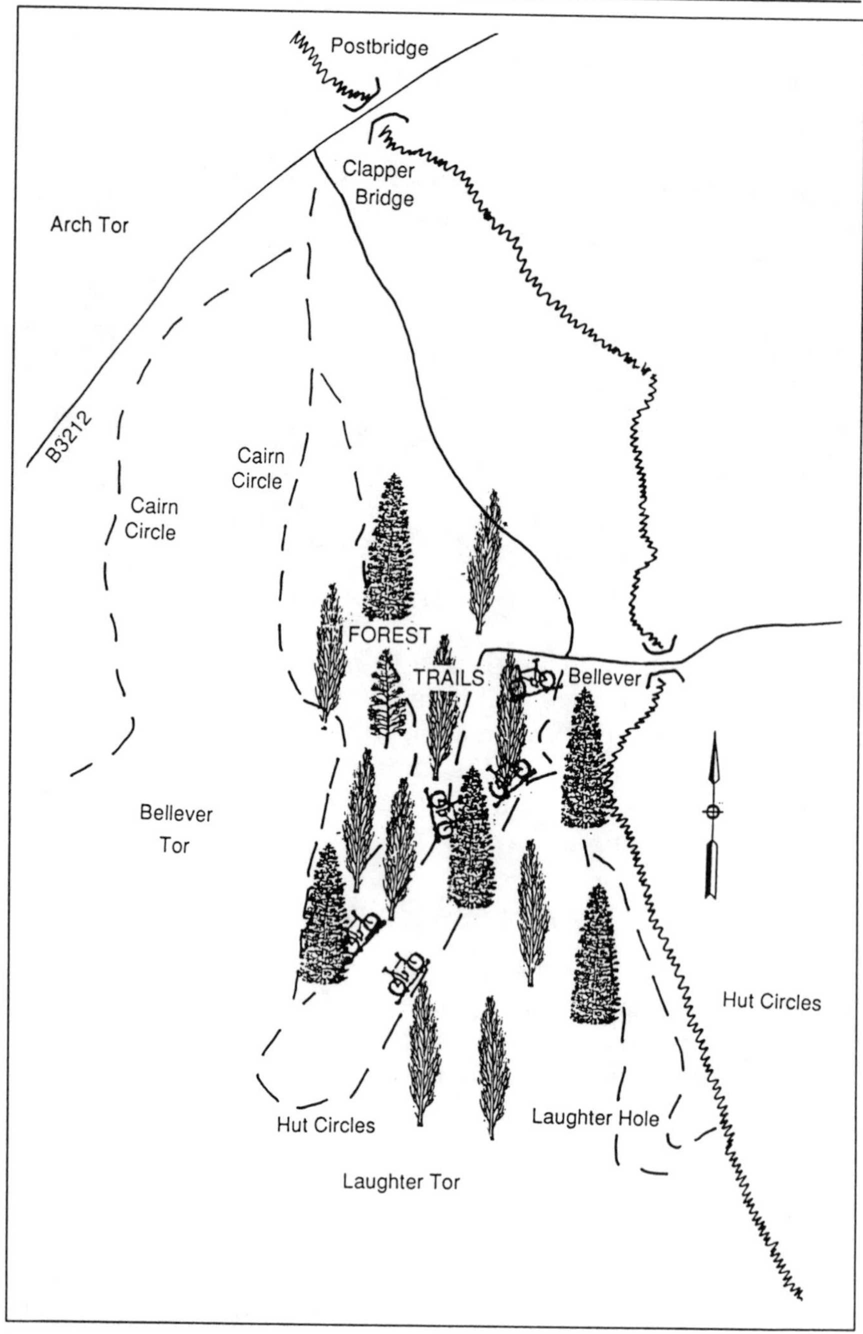
Postbridge
Clapper Bridge
Arch Tor
B3212
Cairn Circle
Cairn Circle
FOREST
TRAILS
Bellever
Bellever Tor
Hut Circles
Laughter Hole
Hut Circles
Laughter Tor

tion boards in the car park. For the less energetic or non-cyclists in your party, a short walk east from the car park will lead to the rock-strewn East Dart River.

Nearby

The nearby hamlet of Postbridge is famed for its stone clapper bridge across the rushing East Dart River. Each of the medieval stone spans is fifteen feet in length. There are guided walks from Postbridge varying in length from about an hour to a whole day. Information can be obtained from the excellent visitor centre in Postbridge car park.

Bellever Tor is one of the highest points in the area at 1456 feet. The views from the top are stunning on a clear day.

Ride 25

Salcombe to Kingsbridge via Inner Hope, South Hams.

An unusually diverse circular ride visiting the pretty estuary resort towns of Salcombe and Kingsbridge and the wild coast at Hope.

Maps: Landranger 1:50,000 series. Sheet number 202.

Distance: Total return ride 15 miles (24 km).

Waymarked: No.

Gradients: A few steep climbs out of coastal points, creeks and coves.

General surface description: Tarmac road and a short section of farm track.

Future proposals: N/A

Other cycle routes linking: N/A

Bicycle hire: Salcombe, Kingsbridge.

Shops and refreshments: Salcombe, Inner and Outer Hope, South Milton, Kingsbridge.

Special comments: N/A

Special warnings: Normal on-road rule. *Be seen!*

Permits: N/A

This diverse ride will take you a full day including a few leisurely stops. It takes you from the peaceful beauty of the Kingsbridge Estuary at Salcombe, past the wild and delightful Hope Cove and through some of Devon's finest little lanes to Kingsbridge before returning to Salcombe, following the estuary past the heads of some of its hidden creeks. This busy tourist area is a horrible place to visit by car. The little lanes are too narrow and the old towns are too congested; if there was ever a perfect area to explore by bicycle, this is it.

Salcombe is set below tree-clad slopes and is situated at the entrance to the Kingsbridge Estuary, five miles south of Kingsbridge. There are interesting shops and restaurants hidden away in the old town's winding streets and near the harbour, which is a haven for recreational sailing and the gateway to endless tidal creeks. Kingsbridge is situated at the landward, northern end of the estuary and has a good range of facilities.

The first part of the route, from Salcombe to Inner and Outer Hope, passes South Sands, an excellent sheltered bathing beach on the edge of Salcombe. You can hire boats in Salcombe and Kingsbridge or try a bit of fishing. Further beauty spots to look forward to include Thurlestone Sands, Kingsbridge and two hardly visited lovely little creeks on the return to Salcombe.

Batson, near Salcombe

Access Points

The chosen starting point of the ride is from the Tourist Information Centre in Salcombe. There is good car parking on the edge of the town by the boatyards but you could start from anywhere along the route. Kingsbridge would be an excellent alternative, especially if you are visiting on a bank holiday or suffering heavy summer traffic. The directions are given in a clockwise direction in deference to the one-way system in Salcombe. There are no particularly difficult right-hand turns.

The Route

1. From the tourist information centre in Salcombe, head along Fore Street (the front) in a south westerly direction.
2. Take the coast road signed Sharpitor and keep the sea close on your left.
3. After the hotels at South Sands, ignore the short road to the museum (unless you want to visit it) and turn sharp right, striking inland towards Combe.
4. At the thatched cottage turn left towards Rew and Malborough.
5. At the 'T' junction, turn right towards Malborough.
6. Take the left turn to Bolberry and Hope Cove.
7. After passing through Inner Hope and Outer Hope, follow the road inland towards Galmpton.
8. Turn right at the junction towards South Huish.
9. Turn sharp left at the crossroads towards South Huish.
10. Turn left to Thurlestone Sands.
11. At Thurlestone Sands, before reaching the sea, turn right and follow the unmade road across the NT car parks. Continue straight on after rejoining the tarmac road.
12. At South Milton, turn left and then right (signed Churchstow and Modbury) to the crossroads at Upton where you should turn right.
13. Continue straight over the B3197 and at the A381, turn left into Kingsbridge.
14. As you enter Kingsbridge, turn right at the traffic island and then right along the minor road between the garage and the dental surgery.
15. Leave Kingsbridge on this minor road towards Ticketwood, on the western shore of the creek.
16. Continue along this road for nearly four kilometres, passing the

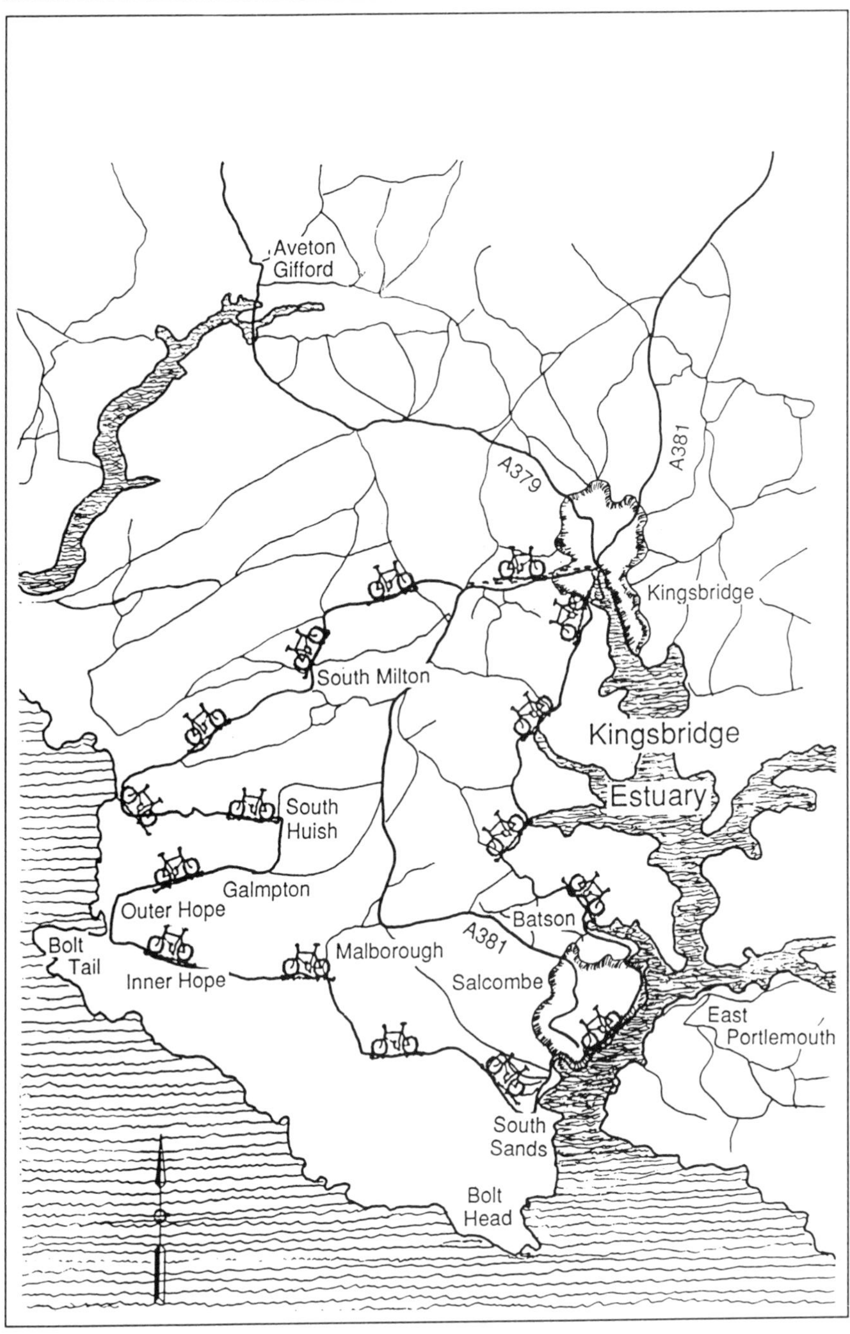
Aveton
Gifford
A379
A381
Kingsbridge
South Milton
Kingsbridge
Estuary
South
Huish
Galmpton
Outer Hope
Batson
Bolt
Tail
Inner Hope
Malborough
A381
Salcombe
East
Portlemouth
South
Sands
Bolt
Head

creeks at Collapit and Blanksmill and then turn left at the 'T' junction.

17. Follow up this hill and then go left at the crossroads towards Lower Batson.
18. Turn right at the three-way junction signed Salcombe and descend into Batson.
19. In the village turn left to follow the creek with the water on your left, follow this road into Salcombe.

Nearby

Bolt Tail is the imposing headland that looks down on Inner Hope. It was first fortified in the Iron Age. It has been the scene of numerous shipwrecks including the 'San Pedro el Major' which strayed from the Spanish Armada in 1588 and foundered here with the loss of 40 lives. The worst disaster at Bolt Tail was in 1760 when the entire 700-man crew of the warship 'Ramillies' lost their lives when their ship ran aground in full view of the villagers of Inner Hope.

Salcombe was the departure point for many thousands of Americans on their way to the Normandy landings in 1944. Their bravery is commemorated by a plaque in Normandy Way.

Ride 26

A Figure of 8: Dartington to Dittisham via Totnes, Bow Creek and Tuckenhay, South Hams.

A superb figure-of-eight ride from Dartington to Dittisham via some of the most glorious parts of the South Hams and the Dart Valley.

Maps: Landranger 1:50,000 series. Sheet number 202.

Distance: Total return ride 26 miles (42 km).

Waymarked: No.

Gradients: This is an energetic ride with plenty of sharp climbs and descents but every one worth the effort.

General surface description: Tarmac on narrow country lanes.

Future proposals: N/A

Other cycle routes linking: N/A

Bicycle hire: Totnes.

Shops and refreshments: Dartington, Totnes, Bow, Dittisham, Cornworthy, Tuckenhay.

Special comments: N/A

Special warnings: *Be seen* on the road.

Permits: N/A

To the west of the Dart in the countryside between Totnes and Dartmouth is an oft-forgotten area of South Hams. This ride traces its route through a network of glorious little high-sided Devon lanes that are laced around this area. Highlights include visits to the charming creek-side villages of Dittisham and Tuckenhay as well as crossing the Harbourne River at Bow Bridge.

From Dartington to Totnes the route follows a glorious (if a little short) railway path which runs alongside the River Dart. Beyond Totnes, the ride is almost entirely on little lanes and byways which, although not completely traffic free, are used mainly by slow moving local traffic and tourists. There are inevitably a few climbs but these are usually rewarded by a good view and the route is very well sheltered if the wind is blowing. There are some great pubs along the way and some delightful out-of-the-way villages to visit.

The ride will take a full day, with time for stops and breathers. Although there is no need to rush, there is plenty to see. If you are planning a full day's ride, Dittisham is very nicely placed for a half-way lunch stop and if you are feeling nautical, motor boats are available for hire from the quay here. There are also foot-ferry boats to the other side of the river and to Dartmouth from Dittisham.

Dittisham

Access Points

The starting point of the ride is from the Dartington Hall Cider Press Centre at Shinner's Bridge, a couple of miles north-west of Totnes. There is good parking here and some interesting shops as well as refreshments and toilets.

The first and last parts of the ride are via a dedicated cycle path. At the time of writing, a small link around Totnes station was incomplete; there is a footpath along the river, which is not officially open to cyclists. This situation is under review and will be resolved in due course. Item 2 in the directions is purposely vague but by following 'Town Centre' signposts or 'Riverside Footpath' signposts, you will arrive at the bottom of Totnes by one route or another.

The Route

1. Follow the waymarked cycle path out of the Cider Press Centre to the station in Totnes. This cycle path runs parallel to the A385 Totnes road via the edge of Dartington Hall and the riverside track.
2. From the station, make your way to the town centre by turning left out of the station and forking right at the first roundabout. This is a busy road section and is partly avoidable by utilising the Riverside Footpath, where cyclists should officially dismount and push.
3. From the square (The Plains) at the bottom of the main shopping area, with your back to the river, turn left via New Walk and then right at the end of the square, passing in front of the Job Centre.
4. Take the left turn immediately past the Job Centre following past the houses and then climbing away up Moat Hill and Totnes Down Hill away from the town towards Ashprington and the south.
5. About 1½ km after the road levels out, you will come to a cross roads. At the 'T' junction, turn left towards Ashprington.
6. Turn right at the cross in Ashprington village and descend to Bow Creek.
7. At the bottom of the hill, do not cross Bow Bridge, but turn right and then immediately left, leaving Bow Bridge House on your left-hand side.
8. Continue along this lane past Bow Mill to a 'T' junction. Turn left towards Harbertonford.
9. In Harbertonford, turn left at the 'T' junction and then after passing over the stone bridges, left again along the A381.
10. After a short climb take the first left turn, signed to Washbourne and Cornworthy.

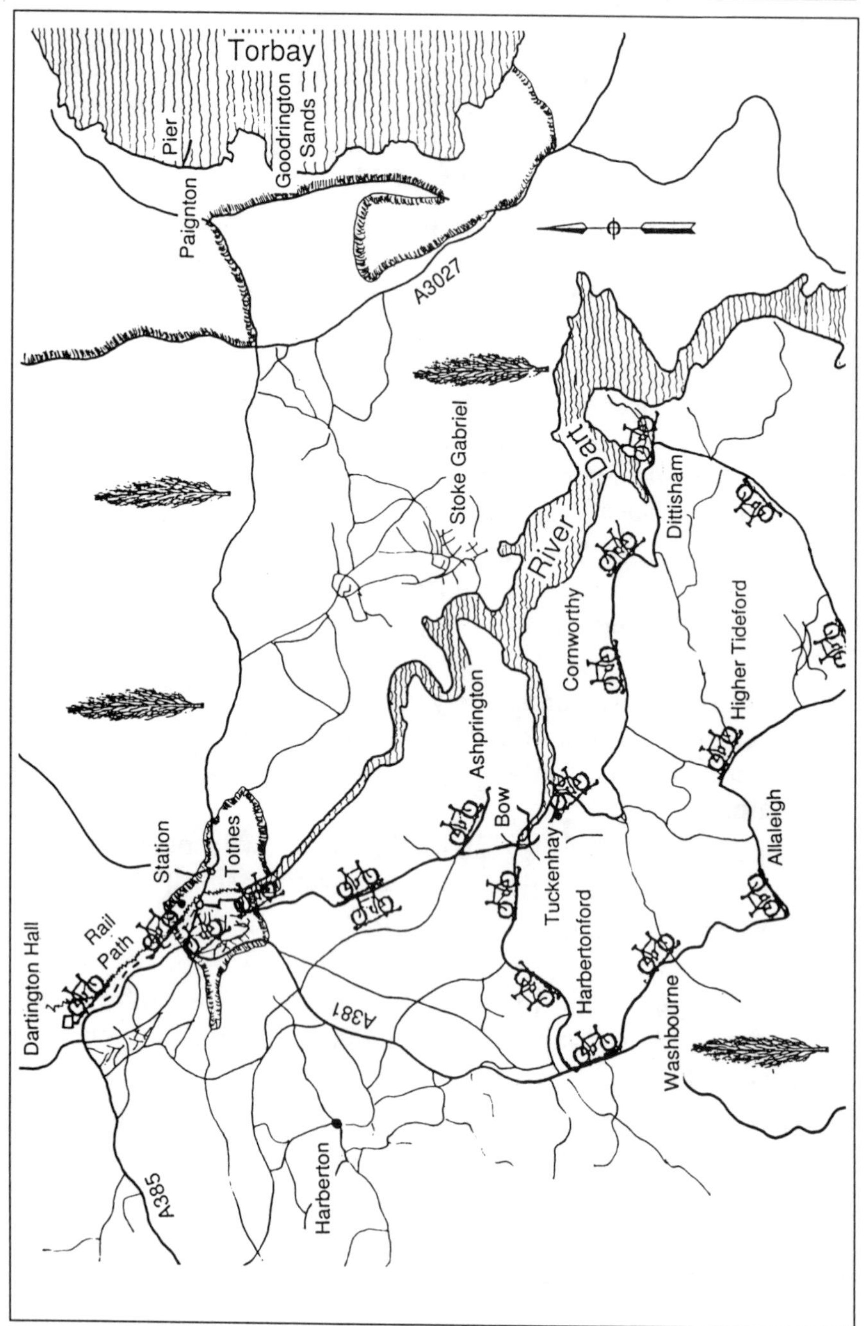
Torbay
Goodrington Sands
Pier
Paignton
A3027
Stoke Gabriel
River Dart
Dittisham
Higher Tideford
Cornworthy
Ashprington
Bow
Tuckenhay
Allaleigh
Harbertonford
Washbourne
Station
Totnes
Rail Path
Dartington Hall
A381
A385
Harberton

12. In Washbourne village, turn right up the very narrow lane by the post box.
13. Turn left along the unmarked lane and follow this road to the village of Allaleigh.
14. At the 'T' junction keep left.
15. At Tideford Crossroads, turn right signed Dartmouth.
16. At the stop sign turn left signed Capton and Dittisham.
17. In Dittisham village, to access the foreshore, turn right either down The Level or down Riverside Road, otherwise keep straight on through the village signed Coombe Cornworthy and Totnes.
18. Continue to follow this road through East Cornworthy.
19. To visit Cornworthy Village turn right at the relevant sign and follow through the village to rejoin this road, otherwise continue following the road towards Tuckenhay. Follow any signs along the way to Tuckenhay Ashprington or Totnes.
20. Continue through Tuckenhay village and to Bow Bridge which you should cross again and then turn left. Proceed straight up the very step hill.
21. At the crossroads, you will rejoin your outbound route. Go straight on to drop down the hill into Totnes and return along your outbound track.

Nearby

The Dart Valley Railway operates a regular steam service from Totnes. Dartington Hall was built in the late 14th century and is now a College of Advanced Education.

Totnes was once a busy inland port. Even today, occasional ships come up on the tide and a steamer service operates from here to Dartmouth. In recent years, Totnes has gained a reputation as an antiques centre.

Dittisham and Tuckenhay are two of the prettiest villages on the River Dart and both worthy of more than a few minutes of your time.

Ride 27

The Exeter Ship Canal: Exeter City Centre to the River Exe Tidal Flats.

An easy, traffic-free return ride from the centre of Exeter along the towpath of the historic Exeter Ship Canal to the tidal estuary of the River Exe.

Maps: Landranger 1:50,000 series. Sheet number 192.

Distance: Total return ride 10 miles (16 km).

Waymarked: Follow the canal towpath.

Gradients: None.

General surface description: Well drained consolidated stone/ash.

Future proposals: General improvement/maintenance. A possibility of a safe crossing across the busy A379.

Other cycle routes linking: A short section of the river can be followed north of the Canal and River Exe Quay through the city. Make sure you are on the west bank. This section forms part of the Exe Valley Cycle Route.

Bicycle hire: Exeter Canal and River Exe Quay and Exeter town centre.

Shops and refreshments: Plenty of facilities by Canal and River Exe Quay plus a superbly situated pub/hotel at the southern, sea-lock end of canal. Another well-situated pub a couple of miles south of the basin.

Special comments: N/A

Special warnings: Beware of mooring spikes and pedestrians along the canal. The unavoidable crossing of the A379 involves a dash across fast-moving traffic including heavy lorries. It is safe enough with responsible adult guidance but unsuitable for unaccompanied children.

Permits: N/A

Starting by Exeter's fascinating Maritime Museum, this ride follows the towpath of the Exeter Ship Canal from the quay of the Canal and River Exe basin just minutes out of Exeter City centre to the peaceful surroundings of the canal's sea lock on the tidal flats of the Exe estuary just north of Powderham Castle.

This superb towpath route offers an exciting and safe recreational ride, a linear park for general recreation purposes and a useful commuting facility for local cyclists. The towpath is surrounded by beauty and rich in colour and scent from a profusion of wild flowers. There is a minimum of contact with motor traffic, although there is one horrible main road to cross, and there are plenty of amenities along the way. As long as care is taken on the very busy 'A' road crossing, this is a safe family ride.

The towpath's surface is ideal for cycling, walking and movement of wheelchairs and because of it follows the canal, enjoys level gradients and a well drained substructure. It offers a 10-mile (16 km) return stretch of virtually uninterrupted easy cycling. Both the novice cyclist or the hardened enthusiast can capture equal pleasure. A novice rider should easily and comfortably cover the route one way in under two hours cycling.

Access Points

The ride is described from the Canal and River Exe Quay by the Maritime Museum in Exeter where there is ample car parking. The towpath can also be accessed from the road island on the A379 just south of the village of Exminster.

Waterside, Exeter

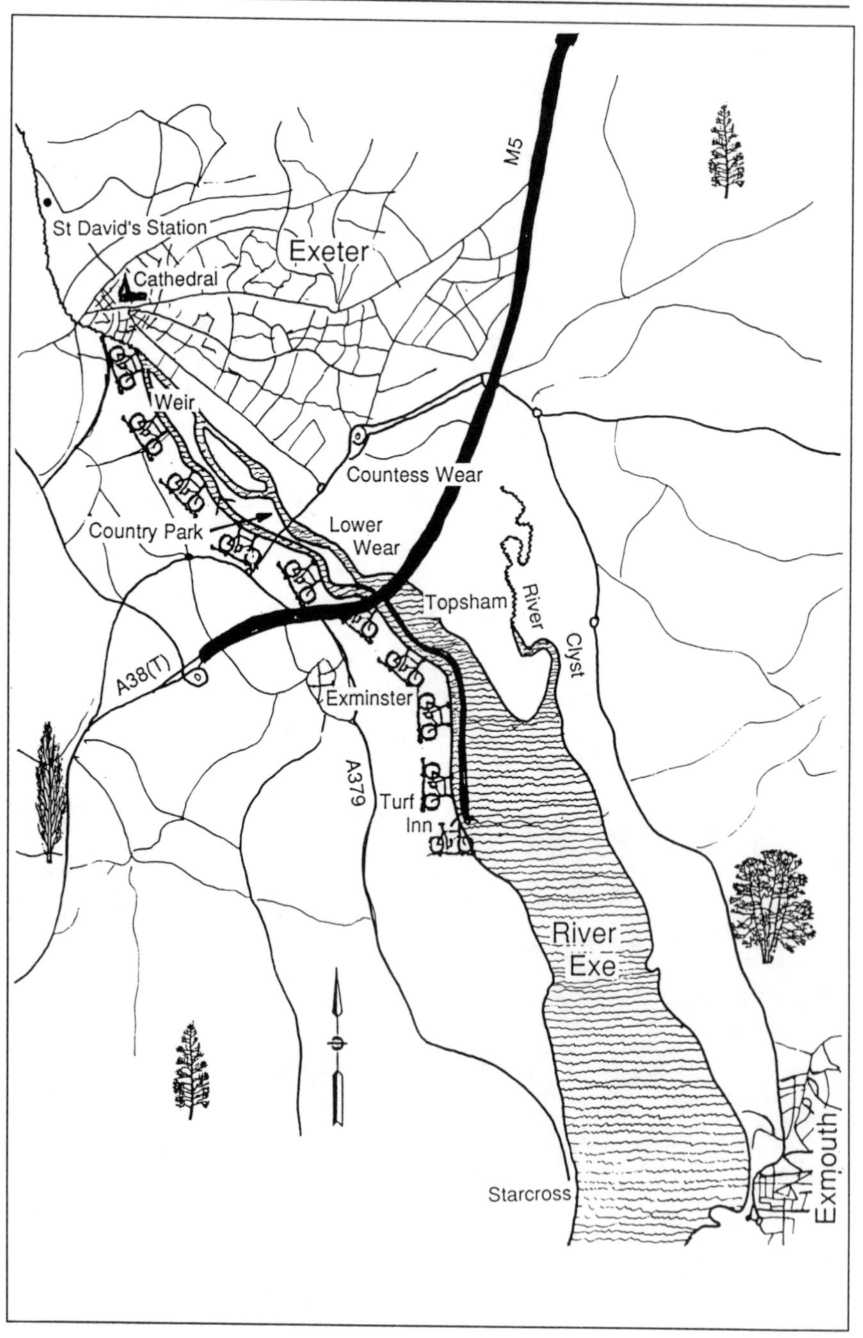
M5
St David's Station
Exeter
Cathedral
Weir
Countess Wear
Country Park
Lower
Wear
Topsham
River
Clyst
A38(T)
Exminster
A379
Turf
Inn
River
Exe
Starcross
Exmouth

The Route

1. From the Canal and River Exe Quay in Exeter, by the Maritime Museum, head south on the western bank of the River Exe.
2. After a short distance, follow the towpath alongside the Exeter Ship Canal while the River Exe flows away to the east. There are a couple of footbridges within a mile of leaving the canal and River Exe quay where you may access the water meadows of the river for a diversion or a picnic.
3. Continue south along the towpath, passing the broad ship lock and the 'Double Locks Inn'.
4. Take great care crossing the horribly busy A379. From here, the rest of the ride is magically peaceful and traffic free. There is a special contrast passing under the vastness of the M5 where you may well wonder why everybody is such a rush. In the last couple of miles down to the 'Turf Inn' you will be increasingly aware of the River Exe widening out on your left. It is possible, subject to schedules, to take a ferry across the Exe to Topsham, accessed by swing footbridge over the canal about a mile north of the Turf Hotel. The ferry point is clearly signed.
5. Return the way you came.

Nearby

The Exeter Ship Canal was originally cut in 1567 and subsequently extended in the 17th century. The reason for the canal was more to overcome a right of way problem than a geographical barrier as 1567 was not the first time that Exeter had been a seaport. Centuries before Exeter had enjoyed a clear shipping channel from the sea to the city centre via the River Exe.

Unfortunately this all came to an end in 1282 when a certain Isabel, the ruling Countess of Devon, rather selfishly decided to build a weir (the Countess Weir). The lowering of the water and the physical blockage of the river effectively closed Exeter as a seaport and a long legal wrangle ensued in an effort by the city's people to reopen their port. Topsham grew in stature for a while as it became the port serving Exeter while matters were sorted out. There was no quick fix for this problem and it took no less than three centuries for the townspeople to win their legal battle against the inheriting Dukedom and only then because the current Duke, Hugh Courtenay, was executed for treason by Henry VIII. When the offending weir was removed it was too late, the damage had been done and the River Exe was irretrievably silted up. It was for this reason that the canal was dug, designed to avoid the silted River Exe and once again allow ships to sail into the centre of Exeter City from the open sea. The canal was an immediate commercial success.

Leonardo de Vinci had used mitre-gate pound-locks for the first time in the construction of the Naviglio Interno in Italy in 1497. The Exeter Ship Canal used the same system seventy years later to become the first canal of this type to be built in Great Britain. From this time on, at an ever accelerating pace, the canal age had begun although over a hundred years would pass before engineers and investors really launched the big push towards a national network.

Ride 28

Mortehoe to Ilfracombe, Devon
(One for the toddlers!)

A two-mile one-way trip along a railway path, through an old tunnel, past reservoirs and into an idyllic broadleaf nature reserve.

Maps: Landranger 1:50,000 series. Sheet number 180.

Distance: Total one way ride 2 miles (3½ km).

Waymarked: Follow the railway path.

Gradients: Uphill or downhill (or both) – your choice.

General surface description: Consolidated well-drained old trackbed.

Future proposals: Constant maintenance of the scrub.

Other cycle routes linking: In the future there may be a link to the Tarka Trail (see ride 13).

Bicycle hire: Ilfracombe.

Shops and refreshments: Ilfracombe.

Special comments: Future proposals may link this ride to the Tarka Trail (see ride 13).

Special warnings: N/A

Permits: N/A

It could be argued that this ride is too short to be included in this collection, but anybody who had witnessed the expression of sheer joy on the face of a seven-year-old as they sped down this old railway path on their little bike, would understand the pressing need for the inclusion of such a ride.

Do not think that this excludes more mature cyclists – on the contrary, if you have only a short length of time to spare then surely this is the ideal way to spend it. What do you do for that last hour before sunset or on that last morning while you wait for the main road and motorway jams to ease before returning home after a bank holiday break? Get the bikes off the car rack and go for it. A gentle uphill pedal to the top and a delightful long freewheel all the way back down again, all in less than half an hour. If you are feeling really lazy, start at the top and send a driver to meet you at the bottom. On arriving there, without pedalling once, put the bikes back on the car rack and do it again. This would surely be the laziest form of cycling known to man, permanently downhill and great fun for kids. It is just a shame that it is not a little longer.

The railway path and the Cairn are managed by the Devon Wildlife Trust. The railway has been long disused and has done a successful job of reinstating itself as a natural wildlife and wild plant habitat, taking best advantage of its non-agricultural status and its shady wind-protected cuttings. The Cairn is an idyllic 19th century plantation of mixed broadleaf and pine conifer. The Devon Wildlife Trust manages the environment by protecting the area and cutting back willow to create a good balance of vegetation types.

Access Points

For the top of the ride find Lee Bridge Car Park off the B3231. To get to this leave Ilfracombe on the B3231 through the village of Slade (from the town follow the signs for Slade Reservoirs) The car park will be seen on your right just before the 'T' junction with the B3343.

Access to bottom of the ride is via the Cairn in Ilfracombe which can be accessed from Kingsley Avenue, off the A361, from Station Road or from the footpath beside Slade Post Office.

The Route

Nothing too complicated here. From the car park at Lee Bridge simply follow the railway downhill to Ilfracombe. On the way you will pass through an interesting old railway tunnel, pass Higher Reservoir and Lower Reservoir and have a chance to stop along the way and soak up the beauty of the surroundings. Starting from Ilfracombe, the trail goes gently uphill to Lee Bridge.

Nearby

There are many rare species of butterfly along the railway path.

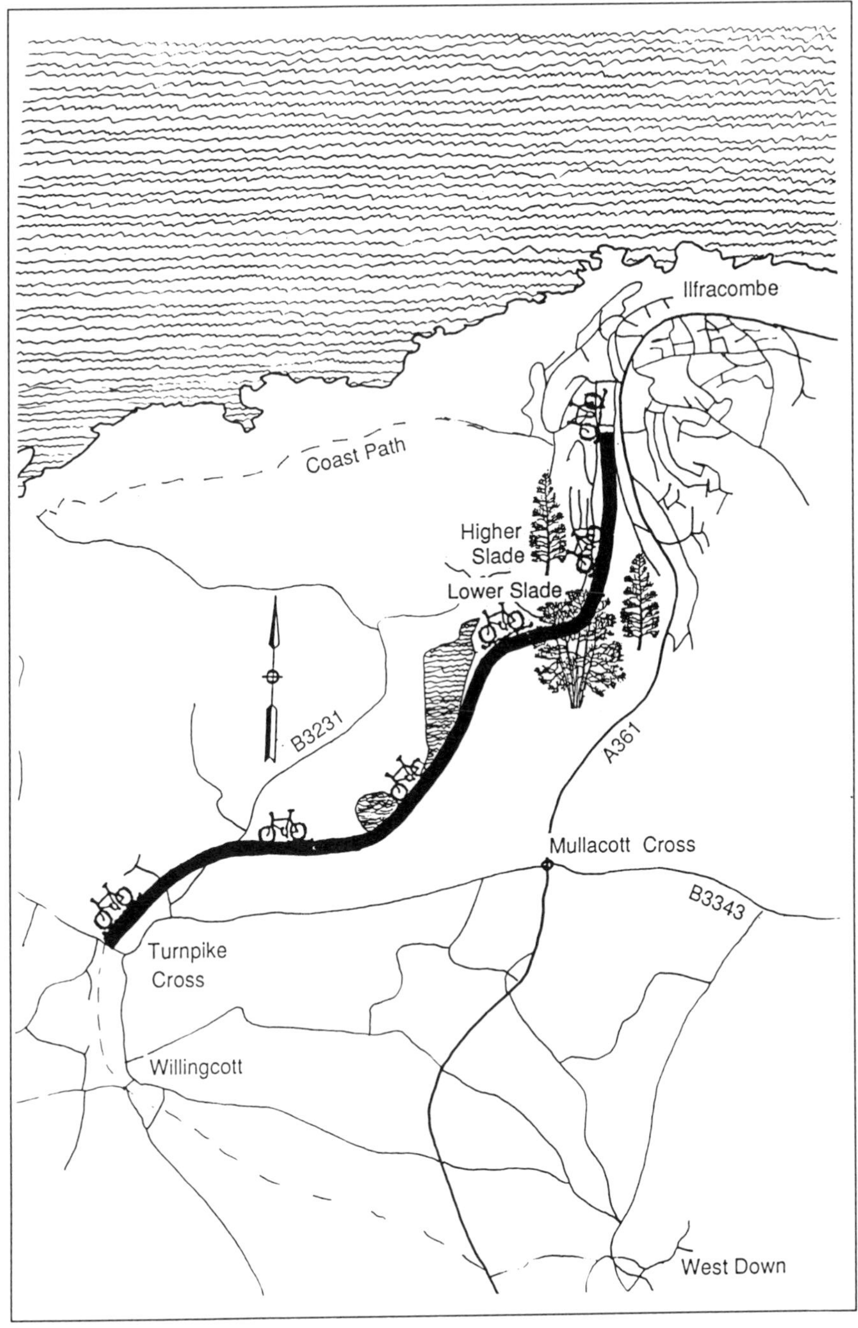
Ilfracombe
Coast Path
Higher
Slade
Lower Slade
B3231
A361
Mullacott Cross
B3343
Turnpike
Cross
Willingcott
West Down

This way to Ilfracombe!

These include Green Hairstreak, Marbled White, Dingy Skipper and Painted Lady. Birds supported by the habitat include jay, buzzard, raven,wood warbler, blackcap and both Greater and Lesser Spotted Woodpecker.

When you arrive at the bottom of the hill you will have a chance to enjoy the shady and lush woodland of the Cairn. Flowering species within the wood include bluebell, sanicle, pignut, dog violet, bugle, moschatel ('town hall clock'), three-cornered leek plus at least three species of orchid. Over 80 species of lichen have been recorded and the whole woodland area is rich in fern. Tree species include the predominant pine, oak and beech as well as Norway maple, sweet chestnut and sycamore. Cairn Top is the 475 foot (145 metre) high rocky outcrop which is surrounded by the 19 acres of Cairn woodland.

Ride 29

South Molton Circular Ride via Heasley Mill and Northland Cross, North East Devon.

An eighteen-and-a-half mile circular ride along the quiet country lanes of east Devon.

Maps: Landranger 1:50,000 series. Sheet number 180.

Distance: Total return ride 18½ miles (30 km).

Waymarked: Sign posts and finger posts.

Gradients: Generally, a steady climb in the first half of the ride rewarded by great views and steady descent in the last nine miles.

General surface description: Tarmac.

Future proposals: N/A

Other cycle routes linking: N/A

Bicycle hire: Eggesford Country Centre. Barnstaple.

Shops and refreshments: Plenty of villages along the route.

Special comments: N/A

Special warnings: *Be seen!* **The ride is on minor public roads.**

Permits: N/A

Set in some of the softest and most beautiful scenery in Devon, this simple route meanders around the valleys of the River Mole and its tributaries north of the lovely little town of South Molton and climbs on to the edge of Exmoor. South Molton has been important three or four times in its long history. First it was a prosperous Anglo-Saxon settlement nestling in the meeting of the rivers. It became a busy woollen centre during the Middle Ages and more recently an administration centre for an active iron and copper mining industry. It was also a busy coach stop en route to Barnstaple to Bideford.

The woollen industry declined, the mines were closed, the coach stopped running due to the competition from the railways and the Anglo-Saxons all died years ago, so all that was left for South Molton was the local agriculture and tourism. The population is amazingly steady at roughly half of the 1850 level.

The River Mole and its tributaries tumble and splash their merry way down their valleys and form a major feature of this route. The cycling is most pleasant and although the steady climb of the first half is acceptable on the solid tarmac minor road surface, it will draw on your energy resources. The rewards are superb views, for which, at many locations along the route, a camera and binoculars will be well worth taking along. There are some very pleasant picnic areas in the woods north of South Molton.

Access Points

The ride is described from the museum. It can also be started from the centre of North Molton. There is good car parking in South Molton.

The Route

1. From the post office in the centre of South Molton, head east along the A361, in the direction of Bampton passing the Medical Hall on the right and the Tourist Information Office on your left.
2. Turn left into Station Road (signed North Molton) and after passing the Pathfields Industrial Estate, follow the road along the tributary of the River Mole through the lush wooded valley. (Cross the main A361(T) with care).
3. Turn left in North Molton village signed Heasley Mill and 'Simonsbath'.
4. Keep left at the next junction signed Heasley Mill and Simonsbath.
5. Keep right at the next fork following the same signed and straight ahead at the sharp left-hand bend signed Heasley Mill.
6. Keep right in the village of Heasley Mill signed South Radworthy and North Radworthy and then keep left signed Fyldon, North Radworthy and Simonsbath.
7. Follow through wooded valley and continue to follow signs to North Radworthy.

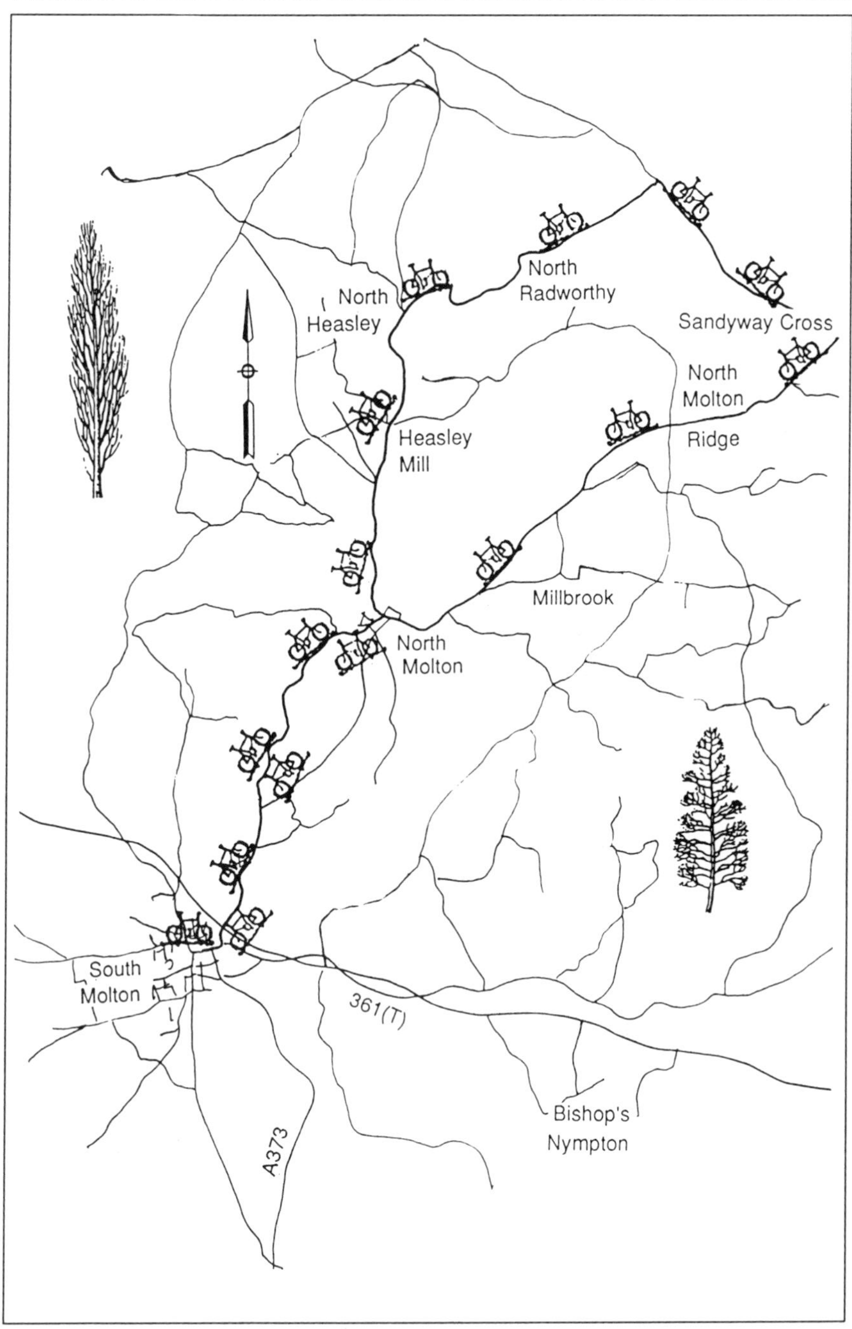
North Heasley
North Radworthy
Sandyway Cross
North Molton Ridge
Heasley Mill
Millbrook
North Molton
South Molton
361(T)
A373
Bishop's Nympton

8. At T junction turn right signed Sandyway and South Molton This is the half way point of the ride. From here the general trend is downwards.
9. Carry straight on along the side of the valley with great views to the right.
10. Turn right at the next junction signed North Molton and Molland.
11. Continue straight ahead following the signs to North Molton and South Molton There are great views to the left.
12. Follow straight through the village of North Molton and retrace your track back to South Molton.

'The George', South Molton

Nearby

There are some interesting disused mine workings and an old mill at Heasley Mill Hamlet just north of the main route, north of North Molton. The museum at South Molton traces the town's prosperous past and subsequent fall into comparative decline.

Ride 30

The River Coly Valley, from Seaton via Colyton.

A circular ride inland from Seaton through Colyford to Colyton and around the beautiful River Coly valley.

Maps: Landranger 1:50,000 series. Sheet number 193.

Distance: Total return circular ride 14 miles (22 km).

Waymarked: No.

Gradients: Very easy going.

General surface description: Minor road tarmac.

Future proposals: N/A

Other cycle routes linking: N/A

Bicycle hire: Seaton.

Shops and refreshments: Seaton, Colyford, Colyton.

Special comments: N/A

Special warnings: *Be seen!*

Permits: N/A

This is an easy and most rewarding circular ride around the lovely River Coly and River Axe valleys visiting Seaton, Colyford and the delightful village of Colyton. Ideal for a very leisurely day or an undemanding afternoon, the ride follows minor roads through these lush and fertile valleys and begins from the tramway station and the sea front in Seaton.

Make a point to have a ride on the old tramway as countless thousands of holiday makers have over the years since it was built. The mile-long shingle beach at Seaton is a refreshing walk, especially on a windy day, and there is always a good choice of fresh seafood for promenade snacks which should be combined with locally-made ice cream to ensure that you go away with the feeling that you have had a real day out at the seaside.

Apart from the straightforward inland trip described here, this is good cycling country. The coastal ride from Seaton west to Sidmouth passes through Branscombe and is a delightful, if somewhat more demanding, ride which may be a good choice on a bright day. A continuation up the Coly valley will take you up into some charming hilly country around Northleigh but again is much harder going.

Access Points

The ride is described from the tramway station in Seaton. There is ample car parking in the two large car parks nearby. The tourist information will have useful information on the area.

The Route

1. From the Harbour Road car park complex, by the electric tramway station in Seaton, turn left out the car park (signed All Routes) and left again at the mini island towards Lyme Regis.
2. After a short distance, turn right into Trevelyan Road leading to the sea front. Follow this road around to the right and proceed along the sea front with the beach on your left.
3. Where the road starts to climb, turn right around the island and back towards the town centre signed Exeter and Lyme Regis. Keep left into the town.
4. Go left in front of the Old George Public House, in deference to the one way system and then right into Manor Road.
5. Turn left at the end of Manor Road into Fore Street and follow this road towards Colyford.
6. Where you see the Colyford name sign on the right, take Popes Lane, the little lane on the left and follow this up to the 'T' junction with the A3052.
7. Go slightly right and straight across the A3052 into Fairview Lane. Follow this road along towards Colyton.
8. At the junction with Hillhead, turn right and follow the lane into Colyton.
9. At the 'T' junction with South Street, turn left.

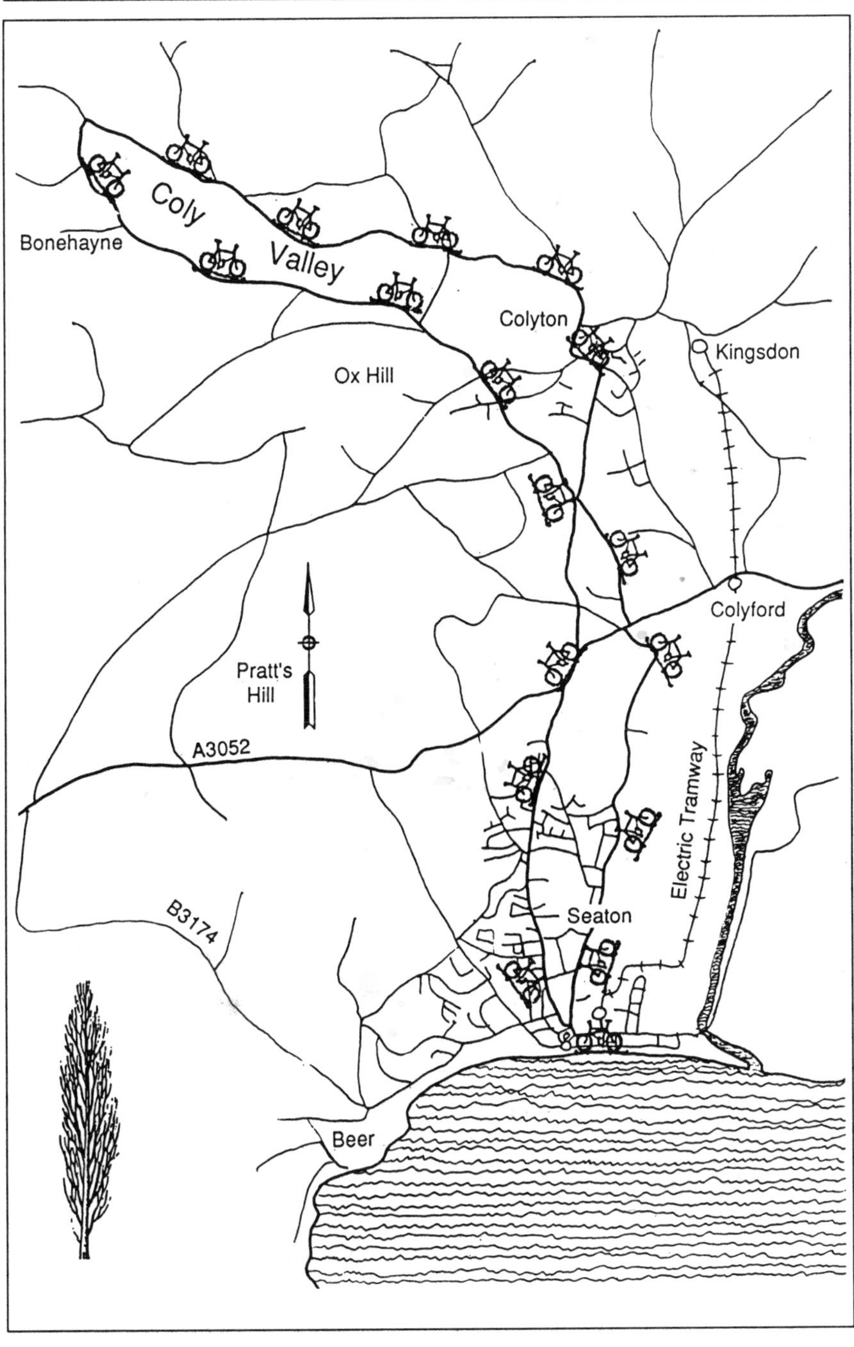
Coly
Valley
Bonehayne
Colyton
Kingsdon
Ox Hill
Colyford
Pratt's
Hill
A3052
Electric Tramway
B3174
Seaton
Beer

Seaton to Colyton Tramway

10. Carry straight ahead into Queens Street, which in turn follows into Kings Street and follow this road around to the right as it winds out of the village.

11. At the road fork after the stone bridge, keep left signed Northleigh.

12. Go left along the minor road signed Bone Hayne Keep along this road to return to Colyton.

13. Back in Colyton, bear left to pass the cemetery on the left.

14. Immediately past the cemetery turn right into the modern housing estate at Burnyards Field Road.

15. Turn right at the 'T' junction signed Seaton and keep left at the next junction following past the picnic area on your left to the main road down 'Gully Shoot'.

16. At the 'T' junction with the A3052, go right for a very short distance and take the first left into Hare Path Road.

17. When you arrive at the one-way system you will be directed to

turn left into Manor Road, which was used to leave Seaton earlier in the ride.

18. Turn right at the end of Manor Road into Fore Street and follow the road around to the left into Harbour Road to return to the car park.

Nearby

Colyton has its roots in 7th-century Saxon times and owes its growth and prosperity to the productive, rich and fertile soils on the lands of the surrounding valleys. The church is notable for an interesting octagonal-shaped lantern top and an Anglo-Saxon cross.

An electric tramway, said to be the only one in the world running open-topped trams, runs from Colyton via Colyford to the seaside town of Seaton. After serious flood and storm damage in 1980, Seaton's shingle and pebble beach is now bordered by a massive sea wall. The town lies at the mouth of the River Axe and has a charming Edwardian and Victorian atmosphere.

Ride 31

Kilkhampton Circular Ride, via the Tamar Lakes, North East Devon and West Cornwall.

A sixteen-mile circular ride along the quiet country lanes of East Devon.

Maps: Landranger 1:50,000 series. Sheet number 190.

Distance: Total return ride 15 miles (22.5 km).

Waymarked: Sign posts and finger posts.

Gradients: Generally, a rolling ride avoiding any major slopes.

General surface description: Tarmac.

Future proposals: N/A

Other cycle routes linking: N/A

Bicycle hire: Bude.

Shops and refreshments: Plenty of villages along the route.

Special comments: N/A

Special warnings: *Be seen!* **The ride is on minor public roads.**

Permits: N/A

Set in some of the softest and most beautiful scenery in Devon, this simple route meanders around the Tamar Reservoirs and on through the lovely villages of Sutcombe and Bradworthy. The River Tamar, in its infancy here, forms the county boundary between Cornwall and Devon and its tributaries enrich the area with lush valleys and green wooded spinneys. Kilkhampton, Cornwall, is a pleasant large village with good shops and a large church, renowned for the vast number (157) of carved bench ends. Its history can be traced back to Saxon times.

The route passes through some delightful countryside, mostly farmland and small villages, as it makes its lazy way into the deep Devon countryside. Industrial archeologists will be interested in the

Quiet back lanes

various structures that are the remains of the Bude Canal (or Bude Aqueduct as it was properly known).

Access Points

The ride is described from the centre of Kilkhampton. It can also easily be started from the centres of Sutcombe or Bradworthy. There is good car parking in Kilkhampton.

The Route

1. From the centre of Kilkhampton, on the A39(T), head south and in the village turn left on to the B3254.
2. Where the B3254 turns sharp right, go straight ahead along the minor road to Thurdon.
3. Turn left in Thurdon village towards Tamar Lakes.
4. After a short distance you may wish to take the excursion from the route to the Tamar Lakes where there is a good interpretative information board.

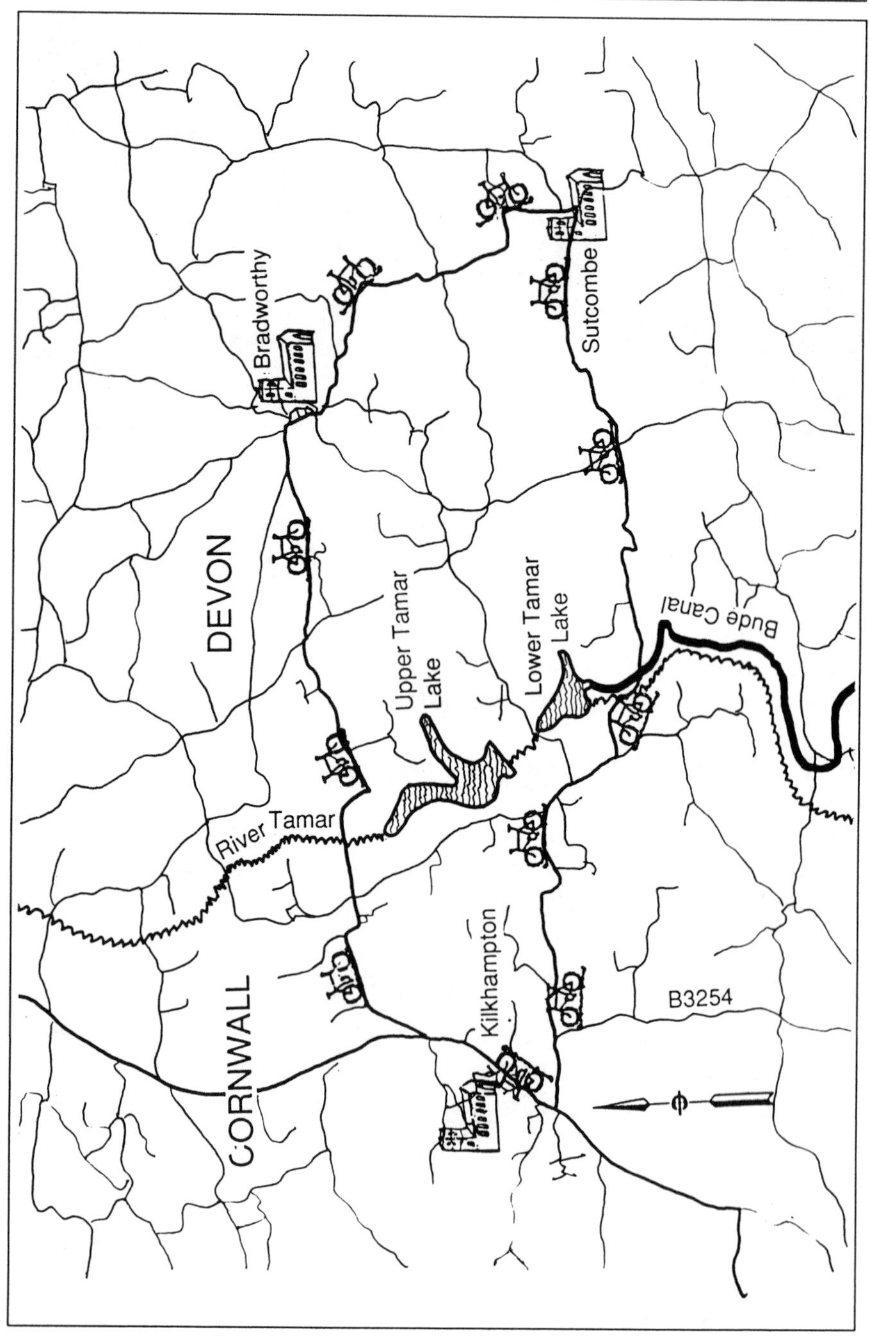
Bradworthy
Sutcombe
DEVON
Upper Tamar Lake
Lower Tamar Lake
Bude Canal
River Tamar
Kilkhampton
CORNWALL
B3254

5. After passing the Tamar Lakes car park, carry on straight ahead (over the county border) and at the crossroads at Soldon Cross, go straight on towards Sutcombe.
6. At Ham Lane junction, turn left for Sutcombe and Bradworthy and cross the old stone bridge into the village of Sutcombe.
7. Keep left at the old stone cross in Sutcombe signed Bradworthy.
8. Continue to follow Bradworthy signs.
9. On entering Bradworthy, keep right at the first road junction and follow into the village square.
10. Turn left out of the square to leave the village past the school.
11. Turn left out of the village on the road for Kilkhampton and Bude.
12. Take the first left turn at the crossroads.
13. Turn right to the Tamar Lakes.
14. Past the lakes, turn right in Thurdon and return along the outbound route to Kilkhampton.

Nearby

The Lower Tamar Lake is the feeder reservoir for the Bude Canal (or Bude Aqueduct as it was properly known) which was completed in 1823 for the purpose of carrying calcium-rich sea sand into the interior for agricultural use. The term 'aqueduct' was applied because the waterway was built on an embankment but in modern terminology, for a waterway to be described as an aqueduct, we might expect it to be supported on some kind of pillar with fresh air beneath, so in this sense, the original name of this navigation may be misleading.

Virworthy Wharf, near the lake, was the last wharf of this system. The inclined plane just to the right of the reservoir is a good example of this method of raising boats. A waymarked two mile walk along the raised canal bed is an interesting departure from the ride.

Ride 32

A Long Tour of Devon and Cornwall.

(Linking all other routes in this book)

Maps: Landranger 1:50,000 series. Sheet numbers 180, 190, 191, 192, 200, 201, 202, 203, 204.

Distance: The full tour, without incidental excursions on to other routes is approximately 300 miles (485 km) in length. There are various options along the way including the possibility of exploring some or all of the other rides and on this basis, this route could form the basis of a two- or three-week tour.

Waymarked: No.

Gradients: Not as bad as some regions but there are plenty of ups and downs, although nothing particularly steep or prolonged.

General surface description: Suitable for any type of bicycle.

Access points: This route touches on every other route in the book. Identify your chosen route by picking out the highlighted text and plan your progress from there.

There are several ways to access each of the individual routes and each cyclist will have his own idea of what is best. Obvious options include transporting bicycles by car, using the various facilities on offer from the railway companies or hiring bicycles near the route. This tour is designed for those of you who wish to explore Devon and Cornwall by bicycle in one overall tour or for those of you who may wish to enjoy a cycling holiday in the area and tour between the various individual routes. To enjoy the complete tour take at least two weeks, preferably three.

This tour makes the best of the individual rides described in this book by linking them all together but because of the greater distances involved and the natural compromise of extended touring, it is not possible to avoid traffic, steep hills or uninteresting scenery to the extent of the smaller tours. Wherever possible the best route has been chosen taking good cycling features into account.

As with every route description, an assumption has to be made that the reader is starting from a fixed point – and for this instance the fixed point has been chosen at Land's End. If, however, you wish to start elsewhere, you will be able to pick up the text at any one of the 31 rides and carry on from there. I have also routed this tour to take the opportunity to visit one or two places that were not specifically explored by individual rides.

Special Note: For Ride 1 – From Land's End take the A30(T) heading west. Turn left along the B3306 to take a short flight from Land's End Airfield. Alternatively follow the directions in Ride 2 to Penzance to access the ship or the heliport.

The Route

1. From Land's End follow the directions for Ride 2 to get to Penzance.
2. From the centre of Penzance head west to Long Rock where you will see a sign to Marazion. Follow the coastal road past St Michael's Mount and through Marazion to join the A394.
3. Follow the A394 to Helston.
4. After exploring Helston, take the A3083 heading south past Culdrose Airfield. Just beyond the airfield, turn left along the B3293 and follow this road to Coverack – Ride 3: the Lizard peninsula.
5. From Coverack, retrace your route to Helston.
6. From Helston, follow the B3297 towards Redruth.
7. In the village of Four Lanes, turn left towards Brea, Camborne and Pool. Follow this road until it comes out on the edge of the built up area of Pool. On the south of the railway line you will find the Mineral Tramways Discovery Centre.
8. Follow the directions in Rides 4, 5 and 6 or check on the latest routes on the tramways at the discovery centre in order to head east to Crofthandy – Ride 4.
9. ... and Ride 5.
10. From Point, head back to the main A39 Truro to Falmouth road and head north east towards Truro.

11. At the village of Playing Place turn right to follow the signs to the King Harry Ferry.
12. After crossing the ferry follow signs to St Just in Roseland.
13. Turn left in St Just in Roseland and follow the A3078.
14. Just before Ruan High Lanes, turn right towards Veryan.
15. From Veryan you can make your way to Pentewan (Ride 7) by following the coastal lanes. In the following order you will pass through Portloe, Portholland, Boswinger, Gorran Haven, Portmellon, Mevagissey and arrive at Pentewan.
16. From Pentewan follow the instructions in Ride 7 to Charlestown.
17. From Charlestown make your way north to the island junction of the A390 and the A391. Take the A391 towards Penwithwick.
18. Join the B3374 to pass through Penwithick and continue to Bugle.
19. Turn right in Bugle to once again follow the A391 and continue to follow this road, crossing the A30(T), to the centre of Bodmin.
20. Follow the sign for Bodmin Gaol and the Camel Trail to join Ride 8.
21. After exploring the Camel Trail and Bodmin, follow the signs for Plymouth. This will take you away from Bodmin on the A389 to the major island/slipway junction with the A30(T). Cross the A30(T) still heading for Plymouth and join the A38(T). After a very short distance take a left turn signed Cardinham Woods to join Ride 9.
22. After exploring Cardinham Woods, make your way northeast through the woods to the village of Cardinham. (OS map sheet 200) From here head east to the village of Mount and from there, continue to head east to the village of St Neot – Ride 10.
23. From St Neot, head south to Dobwalls and the east along the A38(T) to the centre of Liskeard – Ride 11.
24. From Liskeard take the B3254 north to Launceston.
25. Cross the A30(T) with care. After exploring Launceston, take the A388 heading north east. After approximately four miles you

will cross the River Tamar into Devon. A short distance after crossing the Tamar, turn right towards Cross Green and Broadwoodwidger.

26. Just beyond Broadwoodwidger is Ride 12.
27. Follow the route of Ride 12 to Germansweek and from there continue to head east to the A3079. Go left (north west) along the A3079 to the A3072. Turn left along the A3072 and continue to Holsworthy.
28. From Holsworthy take the A3072 heading west and eventually you will come to the B3254. Turn right along the B3254 to Kilkhampton – Ride 31.
29. From Kilkhampton follow the A39 heading north and east to Bideford – Ride 13.
30. Use the cycle route to access Barnstaple and from there follow signed to Ilfracombe – Ride 28.
31. From Ilfracombe, head east along the coast on the A399 north coast road to the junction with the A34. Turn left here to continue east to Lynmouth – Ride 14.
32. Retrace your route to Barnstaple (Also take the A377 south of Barnstaple for Ride 15.
33. From Barnstaple follow the cycle route to Petrockstowe. From Petrockstowe head south to join the A386 and follow this road to Okehampton – Rides 16, 17 and 18.
34. From Okehampton follow Ride 18 to Sticklepath and South Zeal. From here follow the signs for Chagford. The route will take you south through the various lanes. At Chagford – Ride 19.
35. From Chagford, using your compass, head south. There are various routes via a maze of little lanes but by continuing south, you will eventually arrive at a 'T' junction with the B3212. Turn right to head south west across Dartmoor.
36. From Postbridge you can access Ride 24. Continue along the B3212 to Yelverton – Ride 23.
37. From Yelverton head due east through lanes to Buckland Mon-

achorum (OS map sheet 201) and from there through lanes to Bere Alston from where you can access Ride 20.

38. From Bere Alston follow signs and go north through lanes to Tavistock from where you may access Ride 21.
39. From Tavistock head south along the A386 to Yelverton (or follow easy parallel lanes, OS map sheet 201).
40. From Yelverton head south via lanes to Goodmeavy – Ride 22. Follow the ride to Plymouth and the Barbican.
41. From the Barbican, retrace your route to Laira Bridge (A379) and after crossing the bridge heading east, leave Plymouth and follow the A379 to Churchstow.
42. From Churchstow head south to Kingsbridge – Ride 25.
43. From Kingsbridge follow the A379 towards Dartmouth via Torcross and Slapton Sands. Turn right just above Dartmouth on the A3122 to explore the town.
44. Take the A3122 out of Dartmouth and after a short distance turn right towards Dittisham.
45. Return to Dartmouth and take one of the ferry crossings. From the eastern side of the Dart follow the signs to Torquay.
46. From Torquay, follow the coastal route north east to Teignmouth and Dawlish.
47. From Dawlish head north towards Exeter along the A379. Join the Exeter Ship Canal Towing Path just beyond Powderham Castle. (Take little lanes to the right just beyond the castle) – Ride 27.
48. Make your way out of Exeter by heading east along the A3052 towards Seaton – Ride 30.

Appendix: A Selection of Cycle Hire Centres

This is not meant to be a full list. It is included as a supplement and not as recommendation. I know nothing about most of these hirers, except their addresses and phone numbers, which could change at any time.

Cornwall and Plymouth West.

Bridge Bike Hire Trail, The Camel Trail, Wadebridge, CORNWALL. Tel: 01208 813050.

Camel Trail Cycle Hire, Trevanson Street, Wadebridge, CORNWALL. Tel: 01208 814104.

Glyn Davis Hire, South Quay, Padstow, CORNWALL. Tel: 01208 532594.

Hutton Hire, Trevemper Mill, Newquay, CORNWALL. Tel: 01637 851801.

On Your Bike Hire, Hurlingborough Farm, St Agnes CORNWALL. Tel: 01872 552055.

Action Sports, Queen Anne's Battery, Plymouth, DEVON. Tel: 01752 268328

Aldridge Cycles, 38 Cross Street, Camborne, CORNWALL. Tel: 01209 714970

All Trax, Star Garage, Down Thomas, Plymouth, DEVON. Tel: 01752 863272

Blazing Saddles, 29 Killigrew Street, Falmouth, CORNWALL. Tel: 01326 211980

Cycle Hire, Rear of Lloyds Bank, Camelford, CORNWALL. Tel: 01840 770060

Cycle Revolution, Church Square, Bodmin, CORNWALL. Tel: 01208 72557

Cycle Revolution, Eddystone Road, Wadebridge, CORNWALL. Tel: 01208 812021

Cycle Revolution, 7 Beach Road, Newquay, CORNWALL. Tel: 01637 872364.

The Cycle Centre, Bread Street, Penzance, CORNWALL. Tel: 01736 51671.

North Coast Cycles, Ocean View, Bude CORNWALL. Tel: 01288 352974

Truro Cycles, 110 Kenway Street, Truro, CORNWALL. Tel: 01872 71703

Rotary Spokes, 71 Fore Street, Hayle, CORNWALL. Tel: 01736 756973

Pentewan Cycle Hire, Pentewan, Near St Austell, CORNWALL. Tel: 01726 844242

Devon and East

Ivybridge Cycle Hire, Filham Moor Industrial Estate, Ivybridge, DEVON. Tel: 01752 893435.

Bideford Bicycle Hire, Torrington Street, Bideford, DEVON. Tel: 01237 424123

Cycle Hire, 20 Dartmouth Road, Paignton, DEVON. Tel: 01803 521068

Flash Gordon, Old Park Road, off Longbrook Street, Exeter, DEVON. Tel: 01392 213141

Saddles and Paddles, 21 The Quay, Exeter, DEVON. Tel: 01392 424241

Gifford Cycles, 12 Victoria Road, Holsworthy, DEVON. Tel: 01409 254020

Newport Cycles, 65 Newport Road, Barnstaple, DEVON. Tel: 01271 24314

Mark Partridge, Gissons House, Kenniford, Exeter, DEVON. Tel: 01392 833303.

Richard's Bikes, 90 Fore Street, Heavitree, Exeter, DEVON. Tel: 01392 79688

Some Forest Enterprise Centres, Sustrans Centres and Groundwork Enterprise Trust Centres offer bicycle hire. Check with local offices and if all else fails, try the Yellow Pages telephone directory.

More Cycling Books from Sigma!

CYCLE UK! THE ESSENTIAL GUIDE TO LEISURE CYCLING (Revised Edition) – Les Lumsdon *(£9.95)*

50 BEST CYCLE RIDES IN CHESHIRE – Graham Beech *(£7.95)*

OFF-BEAT CYCLING IN THE PEAK DISTRICT – Clive Smith *(£6.95)*

MORE OFF-BEAT CYCLING IN THE PEAK DISTRICT – Clive Smith *(£6.95)*

in The Chilterns

SIGMA Leisure

by Henry Tindell

CYCLING IN NORTH WALES – Philip Routledge *(£7.95)*

CYCLING IN THE LAKE DISTRICT – John Wood *(£7.95)*

BY-WAY BIKING IN THE CHILTERNS – Henry Tindell *(£6.95)*